On the Wings
of Words

On the Wings of Words

of Words

A poetic journal

Lillian Isenberg Rodich

Dedication

This anthology is dedicated to my children: Gail (Richard) Schenck, Carole (Satinder) Bawa and David (Lauri) Rodich and to my grandchildren: Nicole Bawa, Jennifer Schenck, Courtnie Rodich, Alexis (Aaron) Arthur and David (Toni) Schenck.

Their love and support sustain me and their activites in life enrich my days.

On the Wings of Words

on the wings of words
small symbols transported to paper
emotions aroused
senses tantalized
memories awakened
by looking at strange marks
inscribed on a once blank page

Appreciation

It took a circle of family, friends and colleagues to encourage and help me prepare this anthology for publication:

Jackie Wise for her perseverance, patience, computer skills and artistic ability, especially designing the cover, and also submitting the book for publication.

Barbara Tiber for gifting me with her inspiring original collage.

David Rodich for his continuous encouragement and heartfelt belief in my work and for his partnership in the final production of my book.

Leslie Kaplan for her continuous support and encouragement.

Kathy Highcove for her efforts as editor of *In Focus* and (formerly) *The Scribe* in displaying my work so meaningfully and thoughtfully in those publications. Also for mentoring good taste and encouraging me to aspire to high standards.

Ray Malus for his efforts as editor of *The Scribe* in displaying my work so innovatively and generously in that publication and for encouraging me to honor my right brain musings and trust myself.

Douglas Douglas and David Wetterberg for inspiring me with their talents and love of classical poetry and for their careful and expert critiquing.

Sylvia Molesko for her technical advice and patient proof-reading.

Gail Schenck for unique title suggestions.

David Rodich and Alexis Arthur for their complete dedication and challenging work putting the original *Listen Teacher* into print.

Fellow members of CWC SFVs critique groups who have also been supportive, helpful, and inspirational: Rita Keeley Brown, Paula Diggs, Mary Freeman, Judy Garris, Sam Glenn, Clare Goldfarb, Pirhiya Goldstein, Geri Jabara, Norman and Sylvia Molesko, Andrea Polk, Ed Rasky, Erica Stux and Max Schwartz.

A Word About My Grandmother

Alexis Rodich Arthur

I sat on my grandmother's couch staring intently at her, straining my senses to make sure I did not gloss over the cadence of her curated words or allow a carefully crafted metaphor to slip by unnoticed or misinterpreted.

Every once in a while, she'd glance up and offer a brief explanation or back story. She wasn't assessing my reactions; these poems weren't written to elicit one. Nonetheless my laughter and tears could have been a dead giveaway that I was captivated.

Her voice conveys the layered meaning behind each word and although she was sitting across from me, I am sure we were breathing in unison. Her poetry explores life, love, mortality, acceptance, history and tenacity seasoned with hints of irreverence and the perspective only decades of experience can shape.

There is nothing safe about my grandmother's poetry. She writes about some things that might make you uncomfortable, or are dramas of teaching many poor and bilingual children emotionally disturbed and growing up in dangerous areas. First graders in the city of San Fernando living through severe earthquakes, busing, and episodes of gang violence in the 1970's and '80's were under her guidance and protection. Understanding the educational and emotional needs of her students was a huge challenge every day.

She doesn't stick to iambic pentameter, often using "right brain" writing techniques. And a group of poems, akin to hip-hop in their dynamism prompted one writer friend to comment, "pretty good for an old Jewish broad."

As I sit with my grandmother I start fidgeting for my phone. I want to record her reading in her soft, slightly cracking emotional voice. Moments later, I stop and shift my focus to her. No recording could capture her or this moment anyway.

Alexis Rodich Arthur

CHAPTERS

I. *Tell Me a Story* … 1

II. *Did I Tell Him I Loved Him* … 67

III *Listen, Teacher* … 105

IV. *Dancin'* … 155

V. *Streets Scene* … 177

VI. *My Pen Is a Paintbrush* … 215

VII. *Any Way You Look At It* … 275

VIII. *In a Few Words* … 329

Alphabetical Index … 349

Tell Me a Story

my story is an unfinished painting

words searching for a brush

CHAPTER I

Tell Me a Story

CONTENTS

Then and Now 5

Tell Me a Story 6

Legacy 8

Sand....................... 9

Nurturing................. 10

Irises 11

Visiting Vermont............. 12

Vacant Lot, Lost Playground..... 13

Childhood Collage 14

Brother and Sister Pact........ 16

When I Was Ten 18

When I Was Twenty........... 20

When I Was Thirty 22

When I was Forty 24

Beach Party 1950 26

Sailing 27

Decades Rap on My Door 28

Homecoming 1949........... 31

Climbing.................. 32

Morning 33

Senior Years 34

Time Turns 35

Candles 36

Christmas Carousel........... 37

The Clowns Are Here........... 38

Listen for the Laughter........ 39

Generations 40

Once Upon a Time........... 41

Follow Me................... 42

A Golden Moment........... 43

The Pumpkin Patch........... 44

A Child's Eyes 46

Courtnie on a Carousel 47

Alexis at Thirteen 48

Nicole at Five 49

Jennifer at Twelve 50

David at Eight............... 51

Daughters................. 52

Son....................... 53

Innocence................. 54

A Jewish Bride 55

A Wedding Dress, ... 56

Love's Resolutions 58

After Fifty Years 59

Spirit 60

One Day I Will............... 61

Hospitality 62

In Writers' Workshop 63

Rainy Days, Rainy Ways 64

Life's Changing Journey 66

Then and Now

then was then
and now is now

what can be said about yesterdays
except they were once tomorrows
changes take place somewhere in-between

some surprises
some ardently pursued
all of this fascinating
and humbling
sometimes joyous
sometimes devastating

decades ago
could we have imagined
this world as it is now
has the very nature of truth
become an ever-changing mystery

still in all these days and months and years
some things have remained constant
youth has retained
ability to dream and create
and *love* has remained
in our vocabulary

Tell Me a Story

everyone has a story
traded like coins
on a bumpy train ride
spoken in low tones
barely audible in dark dawn's morning

a forgotten operetta
sung through laughter
with notes of pathos

shared casually
over a cup of coffee
and blended into the hum
of strangers' voices

tell me your story
carefully tenderly
guarding your secrets
dictate your story
into a book
with words often overlooked
by those who skim
over the pages
like restless birds

your stories rest
on my bookshelf
holding hands with each other
and nodding through the dust

mountains
echo your stories
where there is no one to listen
and words bounce off
canyon walls

I want to tell you my story
some of it once scribbled
on pages of decades past
some only shadow memories

my pen trembles with effort
words tumble off the pages
denying their own existence
and I search for them
in my dreams

my story doesn't climb a mountain
to reach its summit
or reside proudly and alone
on a book shelf
away from curious spirits

my story is an unfinished painting
words searching for a brush
I am trying
to make peace with it
and find peace within its frame

Legacy

I speak to my parents
for when I lost them
I was orphaned at sixty
now the emptiness returns
I am their seed and once survived
with their nurturing

I speak to my parents
in dawn's stillness
in chaos of noon's crisis
in midnight's moods
their laughter is familiar
their voices echoing
I can see their eyes
feel their presence

I speak to my parents
find comfort in their nearness
reminder of a family
once they were there
often not realizing my insecurities
in the presence of their own

my parents speak to me
continue to provide shelter
beneath their wings
color my memories with continuity
whispering truths in the darkness

Sand

grains of sand
fine as diamond dust
spread like frosting
over the shore

pushed into wave patterns
by a whimsical wind
echoing sea swells
along the beach

endless grains
an eternity of history
written on the edge
of a wordless sea

I walk quickly over sand
before I sink out of control
before my naked feet
burn on my way to the sea

sands are my childhood
diamond dust blown
into peaks and valleys
by whims of the wind

Nurturing

my mother loved plants
not just flowers in full bloom
or yards of colorful beds
like brush strokes in her garden
she cherished the very beginnings
birth of each seedling

my mother saved egg cartons
and tufts of cotton from a large roll
and made dampened beds
individual nests for seeds
she carefully placed in them
then exposed to the friendly sun

my mother tended the seeds
as time went by they germinated
warm and moist in their nursery
soon they cracked open
to reveal fragile green shoots
life had begun

like a good mother
my mother transplanted her babies
to a larger bed and permanent home
rich soil in our backyard
the plants grew strong and tall
and bloomed in brilliance

my mother loved flowers
and tended her plants carefully
she watched seed pods form
and crack open in the dust of summer
tenderly she gathered each germ of life
ready to nurture it once more

Irises

colors ruffled into petals
iridescent and variegated
a fountain
a twirling lady
dancing around golden pillars

follow each footstep
a muddied shoe print
and another
leading to the iris beds
blooms and spikes

translucent purples
golden flowers shaded to brown
each sculpted uniquely
unpredictably
some in brilliant blues and indigo

my mother ordered bulbs
from Germaine's catalogue
picking from glossy pictures
and planting the crumbly beginnings
comforting them with warm soil

beauty harvested much later
with her paintbrush

Visiting Vermont

(Where my mother grew up.)

I visit Burlington
there a blue and purple iris grows
visible in expanses of green

she bends toward the bloom
and cups it gently in her hands
then runs through fields of wild flowers
singing her song off key

Come on you Y girls,
Come on and play with me
And bring your dollies three.
Climb up my apple tree.
Look down my rain barrel,
Slide down my cellar door,
And we'll be jolly friends
Forever more

forever there in soft shadows
mysterious forests
and blueberry patches
in Vermont's delicate summers
and snow-painted winters
she is there her spirit conversing
with whispering trees
her smile greeting wild birds
her fingers exploring soil
feeling seedlings

now I visit Burlington
the wild flowers turn
toward the sun
and I can hear
my mother sing

Vacant Lot, Lost Playground

butterflies brushing my fingertips
illusive dreams I want to capture

I run through tall grass
sticky wild wheat shafts
caught on my sweater
and tangling my hair

like some young animal I leap
pursued or pursuing
galloping with abandon
confronting invincible sunflowers

I trip on a rusty can
and suddenly collapse
into a heap of childhood
on my back contemplating the sky

butterflies brushing my fingertips
illusive dreams I want to capture

Childhood Collage

I twirl my umbrella
and walk in the rain
stepping on mirrors
shattering reflections
dancing to the drumbeat
drops hitting pavement
searching skyward
for silver ribbons
on a dark pillow of clouds

❧

Lon and I built cities
upon the blue and red Chinese carpet
erector set complexes
match stick railroad tracks
salt box buildings
and necktie roads
no one said a word to us
they stepped over the debris
carefully
not one creation disturbed
were Lon and I the anointed ones
incapable of error
and so gifted
our ideas could not be questioned

❧

I loved to play jacks
with all the challenges
an advanced game had to offer
from onezies to twelvezies
one bounce or two bounces
or no bounces at all
a calculated toss
sweep of my hand
across the varnished floor
a ball caught just in time
and best of all
my mother sometimes
joined the game

ೞ

they were simple fairy dolls
fashioned from pipe cleaners
and painted wooden heads
gossamer wings
glowing with glitter
skirts of net and baby ribbon
my treasures my joy to hold
with awe at their glamour
then placed on white enamel shelves
escapees from the dust
in Woolworth's window

Brother and Sister Pact

eating Campbell's vegetable soup
When we're sixty-five, Lionel, where will we be,
You and I …?
Let's make a pact … to remember.

hours minutes seconds
what do we feel
we're children now
these moments are for today

clocks tick
faint outlines in my bedroom
mirrors quiver with night sounds
shadows ease into corners
tangle of thoughts intrude

the train shakes and rumbles
clicking wheels
I'm drowsy
it feels so good
vibrations against my head

Leanne Lockhart's fire place
I can smell wood burning
and hear crunch
of footsteps on wet sand

my hands feel cold
I'm not cold but my hands are
the rings are loose
they twist around with my thoughts
I pick honeysuckle blossoms
and pull the stem through
for a drop of sweetness
while I stroll through early fall leaves

today's clouds
suddenly darken the sky
lightning like a dagger
thunder shakes us with wonder

I feel clouds' heaviness
dampness on my face
on Norton Ave's cracked patio
chipped wooden fence
that's home
always will be

heavy moving clouds
thunder threatens
I sit as a stranger
on the red cement patio
near the broken fence

I'm there still not there
just looking at someone
who's taking my place
and doesn't belong
in my childhood place

When we're sixty-five, Lionel,
where will we be?
Let's make a pact to remember
what our NOW was like.

When I Was Ten

going to Venice plunge
feeling slimy water
all of us splashing
in the smelly green liquid

ballet and tap lessons
dancing shows
on the Broadway department store's
big stage in a small auditorium

Zayda's old Chevy
changing gears while he drove
waiting to sound the horn
holding the steering wheel
until we reached Airdrome Street

walking around my corner
to the grocery store
to buy salt or bread or butter
just one thing for mama
and sometimes I forgot
before I got there

roller skating around the block
feeling vibrations from rough cement
making perfect circles at each corner
listening to our old Philco
Little Orphan Annie
the *Green Hornet Jack Armstrong*
staying home on sick days
with the *Romance of Helen Trent*

Friday mornings
in summer's heat
going to Brooklyn Avenue
where Bubbie could pick out chickens
ugh the smell and cackling

beach days
building sandcastles
chasing waves
digging for clams with my brother

the Orpheum theater on Saturday night
stage shows hosted by Wally Vernon
placards on each side of the stage
newsreels and cartoons
double features and Bingo

an ice-cream soda for a nickel
ten cents for a tuna sandwich
fifteen for a picture show
taking cream-cheese and olive
sandwiches for school lunches
Bubbie packed them in brown paper bags

piano lessons with Mrs. Grayson
I hated them
now I wish I had stuck with it
white cotton panties and undershirts
all home-made dresses
milk bottle curls

jacks and kick-the-can
jump-rope and pick-up-sticks
vacant lots
and tall weeds to play in
when I was ten

When I Was Twenty

walking over the gully to UCLA
the quad lit
by lamp post light stars
twinkling in early evening mist
Janss Steps in a dizzying pattern
leading down to the gyms
studying at night
in Kirkoff Hall
a piano mingling with students' voices

riding the bus to Hollywood
Grauman's Chinese Theater
on Saturday night
my hands exploring
the concrete impressions
in cold reality

traveling by bus
to the May Company Wilshire
windows alive
with Christmas stories
or downtown Los Angeles
and Clifton's cafeteria
its music and pastries and singing waiters
in a jungle of greenery and splashing waterfalls

radio programs on Sunday evenings
Jack Benny and Burns and Allen
my background to study Psychology 203
pancake make-up and white gloves
my own car a blue DeSoto
with disappearing headlights
sunshine lazy beach days
football games and Berkeley weekends

long walks and long talks
with forever friends
optimism in relationships
Hollywood Bowl Concerts
ushering at the Philharmonic
weekend afternoons at the park
at the library at the museum at the zoo

dinner dances
beach barbecues
gentle kisses undemanding caresses
gardenias and long floating gowns
when I was twenty

When I Was Thirty

a real home
with a white picket fence
three children under six
walks to Circle K Market
Gail in a stroller
David and Carole
on each side

love in the afternoon
wearing white short shorts
and a dark tan
feeling desirable
passions overflowing

dirty diapers and sour bottles
someone laughing
someone whining
skinned knees and the feel
of my child's tears on my cheek

bringing a baby home
into a shining nursery
my rocking chair
and an infant
snuggled against me
at three a.m.

coffee klatching with neighbors
little ones crawling
around our feet
trading babysitting
for an evening
to visit and take
a breath of peace and quiet

mom coming for weekends
with her smile and gentleness
soothing away my frustrations

Tupper Ware parties
freshly washed floors
wind blowing through
sheer Priscilla curtains
the smell of babies' nap time

loving my children
my husband my life
warm in the cradle
of the moment
being part of the sisterhood
of young mothers
when I was thirty

When I was Forty

a bouffant hairdo
Loving Care Medium Golden Brown
new identity as a teacher
facing career choices
and home choices once again
relocating and prioritizing

youth elusive
slipping away
rose colored glasses lost
a sudden re-discovery
of the intellectual world
children in high school
and in college
sleepless nights waiting
waiting for each car
to announce its arrival
our front lawn a parking lot

wardrobe hunting a perfect size ten
yellow wool pantsuit
with bell-bottom trousers
less time and more worry
balancing career and home
balancing energy and demands
new friendships
centered away from home

still missing babies' giggles
and sweet smells
weekends alone with my love
Palm Springs Big Bear San Francisco
children taller than I
competing with Scrabble and crosswords

realizing changes
in the mirror's reflection
sometimes feeling out of control
sometimes young spirited as a bird
when I was forty

Beach Party 1950

hi ho come along
we can sing and dance
we can watch
a blazing sun
dunked in the Pacific
and curl our toes
in wet sand

we can light our fire
away from the others
and listen to its crackle
among the sea sounds

Sailing

sailing
in Santa Monica Bay
ripples like smiles in the water
welcoming me

a faint breeze
soft as a sigh
fills the canvas
just enough to glide away

suddenly a dash of wind
powders my face with foam
and salts my lips

I grip the tiller and approach
the corner of the bay
and an open sea becomes
a threatening stranger

the painted sky
brightens my mood
freedom invites me to dare
then a gust of wind
whips the sail
and I race the waves
knowing fear
exhilaration and profound peace
in that moment

℘

sailing
winds guiding
surfing gentle ripples
contentment in moving tides
adrift

Decades Rap on My Door

1953

I need to sort things out
and shout at raging skies,
Retain your rain!
I'm not wise enough
to gather with my loved ones
away from the storm,
its form eludes me.
Diapers and formulas and penicillin…
I'm willing to pray with Spock
and friends on the block.
I need to sort things out,
taking stock of what I've got.

1963

I need to plan a plan
and find out who I am,
which way I ran…
PTA, Girl Scouts, Cub Scouts' smiles
and all the while on trial
for A plus report cards
and perfect style.
I read a book and take a look
forward and backward on the path I took.
It's not a joke to be that broke
and join the ranks of working folk,
then reach to teach, life a peach.
Still can I find the niche
where best I fit?

1973

I need to find the way
to work and play and have my way.
Teens break their hearts
and my heart too … when love is new,
comfort sought in my open arms.
What harms them cuts deep.
I can not sleep.
Driver's Ed…green lights and red.
Camps and cramps
and burning midnight lamps
while my love dreams by my side
and I abide the changing tide.

1983

I need to thrill and rejoice
with each youngster's resounding voice,
shrill and sweet and stomping feet
and throaty volume of lusty cries.
I am wise to realize a grandma's joy;
nothing annoys or destroys my mood.
Smiles are real,
something I can feel.
The love spills over into passion
for my mate
and with pounding heart I wait.

1993

I need to turn my dreams around,
pull back and wonder what it's all about.
Career a word no longer heard,
no longer near or touched by fear,
not this year, just a tear
shed somewhere else, my other self.
A simple flower blooms, I see
room for memories, room for me.
And in the confusion an intrusion
of melancholy is an illusion…
there is life and light in the twilight.

2003

I need to sort things out,
explore a new path
and learn to laugh,
search my soul for comfort,
awaken joy in my heart once more.
Will my spirit ever soar
beyond the grief and pain?
Is there any way one instead of two,
surrounded by a multitude, can learn to feel again?

2013

I need to sort things out and shout,
Hope and creativity are more than words.
They are choices in a landscape of beauty
or a landscape of despair.
There are treasures yet to be discovered
And memories to be treasured
I am not lost
I am not alone.

Homecoming 1949

my head rests
quietly vibrating
with the tremor
of train wheels
a shrill whistle intrudes
upon my voiceless thoughts
I open my eyes and look out
at the vast pacific
its waves trimmed with emeralds
beach sands stretching
toward a rocky shore
meeting frothy swirls

I smile to myself
content and lulled
into a wakeful dream
thoughts of Berkeley
and independence
challenges and rewards
all mingle with visions
of wildflowers
now whirling past me
and grassy bird sanctuaries
floating out of view
as the wheels click rhythmically

I'm coming home from college

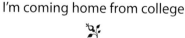

Climbing

once I climbed a mountain
a hill really with rocky paths
still the trail was steep
and my shoes slippery vehicles

I had no time
or patience to notice
delicate wildflowers
peeking through crevices
and nodding in the wind
some crushed by my struggling boots

it was a long hike
up the dusty rock trail
sometimes my fearful clutch
pulled up small plants
not anchored securely enough
along the path's borders

when I stopped
to catch my breath
in a dizzying moment
off balance yet exhilarated
I looked up
and was blinded by the sun
mesmerized by a rainbow of colors

the trail I was following
turned and disappeared
I had almost reached the summit
there I decided
I would sit down and rest a while

Morning

dawn is a crack
silver and pink
misted gray in the darkness
thoughts quiver
into consciousness
in deepening circles
pushing away debris of dreams
teasing reality

sights and sounds
invade my room
fingers of light creep across walls
a train whistle wails
birds converse on nearby branches
I stretch reluctantly

coffee perks automatically
aroma enticing me
I glance at my sleeping lover
grateful for his peaceful presence
snug in my moment of solitude
I rotate slowly
sitting until my world
comes into focus
I begin the day

Senior Years

it's a fine time
a trying time
a lonely time
and one of discovery

it's a frightening time
a frivolous time
a time of denial
and spurts of purpose

it's a peaceful time
a troubled time
a tender embrace
of elusive lovers

it's a painful time
a time of choices
lacking choices
and uncertain pathways

Time Turns

hours and days circle
around and between
lingering memories
songs that echo
in my thoughts

now it is time

to smear paint on canvas
like a child
in a swirl of colors
a sense of joy
without restrictions

to renew replenish
and also abandon
allow dreams to grow
into reality

to visit the sea
build sand castles
not waiting
for a summer's day
to read uninterrupted
for a week
savoring each word
while the dust settles
where it may
each day

it is time
to cherish the moment
dance and write and paint
speak heart to heart
with kindred souls
enjoy roses in my patio
when other gardens
are too far away

Candles

a Christmas tree's
moist green branches
support candles
glittering in my neighbor's window
and reflected in a wreath of good will

eight Chanukah candles
each kindled by the Shammash
and greeted by children singing
relating tales of anguish and triumph
survival of my ancestors

crystal and champagne
candlelight reflected in loving eyes
hands held across a table
in the glow a promise made to be kept
one rain drenched December eve

one hundred birthday candles lit
combined in a blaze of glory
Zayda begging the youngest guests
to help him extinguish each tip of flame
celebrating a century of life

lonely candles burning brightly
in remembrance of our deepest losses
lighting dark corners of grief
continuity in life's circle
treasured flames never extinguished

symbolic candles lights of hope
ignited in classrooms of a ghetto school
students' eyes glowing with discoveries
teachers amidst Asia's turmoil and Africa's strife
holding fragile tapers up to the black draped night

Christmas Carousel

the carousel turns
while Christmas lights greet the night
and painted ponies prance to nowhere
on enchanted silver poles
and magic tinsel of children's laughter
fills midnight's hour
with their innocence and joy

now it is time
to reach for the golden ring
share its bounty
with those whose tears
wash over their smiles
their souls starved
and immune to joy

it is time
to share our treasures
and our hope
before the gears
grind into silence
and the glitter of laughter
is covered with dust

it is time
before the ponies cease to gallop
and the music stops

The Clowns Are Here

clowns are here
make way for laughter
up-side-down smiles
a blue tear caught
halfway down one's cheek

watch another's floppy hat
laughing in the wind
wilted flowers in tears
ah such tender teasing
pantomime stories
spun from air

yellow hair made of straw
painted lashes like spider webs
huge shoes dancing
along a tight-rope
painted on pavement
balloon gloves waving
in awkward balance

listen for children's laughter
and an old couple's chuckle
for they understand
they are healed
by a silly clown's antics

Listen for the Laughter

listen for the laughter
bubbling over a child's playground
hidden in ladies' luncheon chatter
muffled in darkened movie theaters
roaring in smoke-filled taverns
quietly responding to a book
chuckles in fond remembrance

listen for the laughter
coloring ordinary words
shattering tension
releasing tears

Generations

Bubbie crocheted lacy doilies
patterned in cobweb designs
cream colored
over a faded brown sofa
over mahogany tables
smiles in the cold dawn
of a dark room

Nicole counts stitches
winding thick yarn
around her finger
grasps a large hook
pulling tight

a thick pad of purple and orange
under a crystal vase
next to her great grandmother's
fragile doily
in the dusty sunlight

Once Upon a Time

once I was the mother
new to sounds and smells of an infant
running my fingers over velvet skin
clutching a feverish body to my breast

I was once the nurturer
drying a torrent of tears with my apron
driving to the hospital at three a.m.
reading story books to sleepy children

I was once the teacher
drawing a square singing alphabet rhymes
rolling a ball tying a shoelace
introducing books as new friends

I was once the counselor
listening to stories without comment
commenting when I needed to
guiding by example and prayer

I was once the mentor
renewing my own talents
questioning and growing
hanging on through misfortune

once I was the grandmother
new to sounds and smells of an infant
running my fingers over velvet skin
clutching a feverish body to my heart

Follow Me

follow me
grandchild of my life
this hand is extended
and within your reach
I am old of flesh
not of spirit
my hand is strong
and eager to hold yours

come with me
I want to share my treasures
and treasure them more
through your eyes

A Golden Moment

in splintered sunlight
and wind sharp
with uncompromising chill
we feel
exhilaration and warmth
greeting adventure
beneath a leaden canopy

hands and hearts
held in unison
a moment of joy captured
frozen in time
in the chilled landscape
Alexis and Courtnie
Grandpa and Grandma
one Christmas in Maryland
a golden moment

The Pumpkin Patch

chill shakes us and mixes with laughter
Courtnie Alexis and I crunch through dried grass
and open our mouths to the wind

pumpkins roll in the sawdust
their orange faces grooved and scarred
topped by jaunty green caps
I want that little baby one
just as big as my hand Courtnie chants
*then I want **that** one*
and I see a candy-smeared face
peeking around a sixty pound giant
*I want **that** one.*

bells ring
tinkling silver bells
we look over toward mushrooms of dust
where Indians pound out their rhythm
on beaded drums
as they begin to dance
their chant beckons us to join them
eagerly we do
Alexis Courtnie and I skip into the circle

Courtnie's face is painted
a bright feather quivers in her hair
while drum rhythm captures us
and we move into the dance

pumpkins roll in the wind
and we hop over little ones
while our dancing circle grows larger

steps are simple
stamp walk walk stamp walk
and we turn
toward the hot apple cider
toward stacks of corn stalks
toward a sea of pumpkins
alive and glowing
rippling in the wind

then we look up
at a purple and gold sky
diamonds shining in the dusk
and there
in the middle
the largest round orange pumpkin
of them all

A Child's Eyes

wonder in a child's eyes
is unclouded and innocent
of judgment
simply a window to the world
washed clean by brief tears
left in brilliant hues
reality framed
by dew-dipped lashes

Courtnie on a Carousel

your face shines
in the blinking lights
and hands as smooth
as a silken whisper
caress your pony's
mustard colored mane

a painted carriage
full of awe and smiles
follows exactly
one pace behind

sharps and flats travel
hammers on metal strings
you slide down
then rise again
to an occasional sweet note
blooming in strident tones

trees and park benches
pirouette around you
around your laughter
around the yellow-maned
pony you ride
faster and faster
to blur your vision
and send the musical notes flying

Alexis at Thirteen

the slate of a winter sky
and dawn's green sea
swirl in her eyes
reflecting innocence
intelligence
honesty
and a glint of curiosity
her brow is high and smooth
framed by the glow
of tawny hair

she is lean of body
generous of spirit
graceful animated
living the poetry of life

her words are her heart
and speak
with the voice of a woman

Nicole at Five

Nicole's eyes are almond shaped
and dart from here to there
seeing all savoring all

she plays with words
clapping made-up poems
singing to her dolly

she turns and turns
just to feel
the world spin 'round

Nicole delighted by every sense
and spicing each moment
with laughter

Jennifer at Twelve

your eyes twinkled
the first time we saw you
only hours old
and trying to focus
in the cold bright nursery

then emerging beauty
large brown eyes
shining with curiosity
your eager smile
with its illusive dimple

you charmed us all
with your fragile complexity
and simple warmth
a year old and you sang
nursery rhymes by yourself

Jennifer now the child within
shines with womanly grace
and a teenager's curiosity
remembering the puzzles of babyhood
hours putting each piece in place

Jennifer is twelve
challenging computer games
and criminal mysteries
listening to the latest singing stars
crafting greeting cards
and stringing jewels into her story

David at Eight

David is all grown up
or so he feels and acts
his eyes tell you
and his fearless heart

he loves to fish and swim
and figure things out
enjoys a competitive spirit
likes to play games
sometimes paints and writes

David loves those he loves
with passion and loyalty
a face of joy
conquers his pain
and smiles given as a gift
brighten my day

Daughters

you stroll
among sheltering trees
and your feet follow
a man made path

you pause and search
the sculpted branches
gathering sunlight and warmth
along with them as their gilded limbs
gain strength

leaves and blooms painted
into a verdant background
a classic portrait
alive and dancing with shadows

you gaze into their mirror
and begin to recognize yourselves

Son

a miracle arrived
full meaning not realized
in the haze of flowers and hushed voices
in nervous phone calls
unexpected and uncontrollable tears
their glisten constant on
our flushed cheeks

a stranger in our lives
wrapped in a blue blanket
and pulsing with life
filling our hearts with fear
cold nagging fear
and happiness never before experienced
we are responsible
our hearts vulnerable

a miracle as we
journey through life
someone who joins us
someone who changes our lives forever
and makes the journey exciting
and enjoyable
and filled with love
and all the sweeter

first born

Innocence

do you see what I see
as your cheek brushes mine
and your protective arm
is placed lightly around my shoulder

do you gaze at the same wonders
are you in tune with my music
does your pulse beat with my heart's rhythm
are we singing the same song

for we are children of dawn
our love is filled with sunlight
our hearts are pure and uncomplicated
we are bound by silken threads
of innocence

A Jewish Bride

hushed voices
silence washes over
satin and flowers
and my mother's tears

part of me stands far away
like a ghost
hovering over us
while we cling to each other

our heads bend in prayer
we seem to be strangers
a shimmering picture
lacking reality

until
my veil is lifted
and we taste in turn
new sweet wine
while the ghost has
disappeared

and the glass is shattered

A Wedding Dress,

an almost true fairy tale

Once upon a time many many years ago in the province of Larchmont in the Greater Kingdom of Los Angeles a young prince and princess fell in love. From the day they met, they knew they would marry.

The bride wanted a beautiful gown for her wedding. The very first gown she looked at spoke, "You must choose me above any other and keep me near you for many moons and suns, storms and days of sunshine. And I promise you I will bring good karma and love to all those who touch me. Please do not forget this special promise. And only reveal it to those born of your love."

The princess was taken by surprise by all this chatter. But after all she lived in a fairy tale and didn't doubt the words she heard.

"Remember," the dress said, "you must keep our secret for sixty years."

The princess smiled and tried on the dress. It formed to her figure as though it had been made for her. Its beautiful satin gleamed, the net trim was soft and sculptured, and a row of perfect tiny satin buttons marched all the way down the back.

The prince and princess married and found, with each other, the deepest happiness they had ever known. The bride placed the dress, wrapped in dark blue tissue in a special box, and kept it in a safe place. Soon the young couple became king and queen of a new province called Chatsworth.

As years passed, the box was moved around frequently. Still the queen looked at the gown now and then and always returned it to a safe place. The tissue wrinkled , the box dented, and the strange voice never spoke to the bride again. Sixty years passed and the queen felt it was finally time to give her beloved gown away. For, indeed, they had both kept their promise.

But then, the king and queen's first granddaughter fell in love with a wonderful prince. And just for fun the young princess decided to try on the wedding dress. It fit her body perfectly. She twirled around in front of the mirror and felt pure joy embrace her. The satin shone in spite of its wrinkles and the tiny buttons marched down the bodice in a perfect row.

When the smiling queen quietly left the room, she could hear two voices whispering and she knew exactly what was being said.

Love's Resolutions

Yin and Yang
Shadows and Sunlight

winter and summer
loss and treasure
conflict and resolution
tears and laughter
memories and erasures
boredom and passion
discord and harmony
confusion and clarity
showers and rainbows
silence and conversation

separate hearts entwined
and grown into one

After Fifty Years

holding hands
holding hearts
singing silently
sharing champagne
slow dancing without music
mingling tears
mingling laughter
happy talk
sad talk
serious talk
silent talk
lovers' talk
re-discovering each other
at peace
challenges and rewards
forever bonded

Spirit

aging is spirit
willing a body
sometimes unable
to do its bidding

understanding acceptance
long range view
showing solutions possible
when
a misty future swirling
around my feet
suddenly becomes my present

I feel hunger and thirst
for joy and laughter
love and camaraderie
sweetness of summer fruit

aging is quiet times
reflections in a pool of solitude
and one last spirited dance
in flickering firelight

aging is being lost
in a place never anticipated as reality
an unfamiliar face and body reflected
in a full-length mirror
not revealing
unchanged feelings inside

One Day I Will

one day I will
dangle diamond earrings
perm my hair
walk barefoot all day
find my long-ago lover
say Goodbye
and say Hello again

visit my father's grave
play in the snow
drive to Big Sur alone
laugh out loud
smile at a caterpillar

throw away
and gather again
cover my mirrors and walk in dust
quietly without making clouds

one day soon I will

Hospitality

come on in
it's dusty here
construction turbulence outside
still you're welcome
dim moonlight smiles
through streaked windows
on tired nights
and newspapers a week old
coffee stained chronicles
are slippery on worn rugs

chiming clocks not synchronized
may surprise or delight you
dissonant tones behind our laughter
a nail shows in cracked molding
cobwebs ease into shadows
drapes are faded in uneven stripes

come on in
we have coffee brewing
soda crackers and cheese
sink into our sofa and reach for a snack

open our drapes unlock the screen
twilight enters a red and purple hour
it's dusty
you can see particles glisten
flecks of gold floating

wade through the debris
hugs and kisses
rest a while on our worn couch
here's a pillow for your head

In Writers' Workshop

faintest melody
barely audible
distant stereo sings

chirping
thin voices
arguing among branches

jarring note
refrigerator
buzzing on
rumbling off

airplane motor
pulsing humming
disappearing

soft whir
overhead fan
pen scratching
concentrating on paper

sighs
translating thoughts
into written words

Rainy Days, Rainy Ways

After the Northridge Earthquake 1994

It's the merry month of May and not supposed to be raining. Not on my cracked and scarred condo, not on the roses smiling up at a gray sky, not on the dried out cement so recently shimmering in the heat. But rain it must to quench our thirst, to wash us clean of sorrow and debris, to allow the coming cumulus clouds access to a freshly painted sky.

Into every life a little rain must fall. The phrase dances around in my brain as I sit curled up on my couch and stare through our cracked picture window at the splashes of water swirling around pots and patio chairs. Somehow this rain soothes my turbulent soul and confides the promise of better things to come. Streams of water satisfy the thirsty earth and gray skies become a blanket of consolation while sadness begins to fade.

I have known joy in the rain. The smell of wet earth. The comfortable patter of drops on the sidewalk. Twirling my umbrella and doing a splash dance on my driveway. The enchanting sight of a rainbow as I rode home from Palm Springs, my lover's proposal in the front seat of his truck — rain slicing all around us — sunlight glinting through the windshield. Endless afternoons when the kids were little and we all sat warm and cozy in our tiny den and played Monopoly or Pick Up Sticks and drank hot chocolate. School days at Morningside, smelling damp sweaters and the faintly camphor odor of mothballs when I greeted my students on a stormy morning. Playing Heads- up - Seven-up and laughing with the children. Rainy days so many years ago with my best friend Helen Weinblatt, splashing down Ogden Drive, sharing an umbrella, tasting the sweetness of raindrops on our tongues. Walking beach sands in a misty rain, holding hands with my guy, watching a muted sun sink into the grayness, feeling the damp sand between our toes, suddenly breaking into a chase and falling into each other's arms overcome by exhaustion and laughter. Sitting in our daughter Gail's home watching the lightning illuminate silver sheets of water, having Jennifer cuddle up beside me and say, "Grammy, are you scared?"

Rain has framed sad memories and mixed with unshed tears. Standing by my father's grave, unable to comprehend that he was really gone, unable to bear the fine needles of drizzle on my eyelids and forehead. Rain again in a sudden cloudburst when my beloved nephew Barry left all of us in a flood of anguish we thought would never wash away. Saying "goodbye" to my first real boyfriend and mourning what might have been when the sky suddenly darkened and rain began to splatter on my window pane. The floods of 1938 frightening me, muddy water swirling around our Chevy's tires, the streets like rivers and my father carrying me across, my head buried in his neck. Flash floods on our way to Las Vegas heading for higher land, my heart beating so hard I couldn't swallow and my love laughing up at the black clouds and shouting taunts at the thunder. The steady drumbeat of rain while waiting by telephones and in hospital rooms, and praying without words and without the comfort of sunny skies.

Can the rain cleanse the sorrow from my soul, bring its sweetness and healing power into my perception, lull me with its special music and clear the marred canvas of earth and sky?

It's May … much too late in the season for rain. Still the birds are soaring through the mist and singing their joy and the leaves and flowers are glistening.

Life's Changing Journey

life like a carousel
turns and turns
the landscape spins by
blurred in detail
still music surrounds us
remains bright and tinseled
we can hear it in our memories
lyrics to old songs
long ago feelings reawakened
misty pictures come into focus
and smile into our everyday lives

life's carousel journey continues
unfamiliar places come into view
rhythms and melodies change
new words tumble into old songs
new friends wave their untold stories
old friends appear
brightly and forever
and the horses gallop on

CHAPTER II

Did I Tell Him I Loved Him

I'm not sure just when or how

I said those words

CHAPTER II

Did I Tell Him I Loved Him

CONTENTS

In Mourning 71
I Try to Remember 72
Grief. 73
The Path. 74
Autumn 76
Regret 77
Loneliness 78
Solitude 79
p.m. – a.m. 80
Reflecting. 82
Voice of the Sea 83
Lost Lover. 84
A Visit. 85
(Life's) Journey
    Through the Redwoods 86
Serenity 87

Whispers 88
Appointment 89
Unforgettable. 90
Coffee. 91
The Box 92
Clay Dancer 94
Remembrance 96
Changing Times 97
Blossoms in the Sand 98
Night Winds 100
Falling Leaves. 101
Awakening 102
Recovery. 103
A Time to Laugh and
    A Time to Weep 104

In Mourning

it's been ten years
and the tears
are still there
everywhere
they rain upon
my bright parade
and though I stay
within the lights
of optimism
their prism remains
a rainbow I know lies
beyond dark clouds
blown aside

and I abide

I Try to Remember

I try to remember
when evening melts into darkness
window frames shudder
in a lonely gust
voices mumble without words
and shadows invade my solitude

I try to remember
the curve of your smile
feel of your arms around me
blanket of subtle scent of you
echoes of tenderness
your laughter

how every day was an adventure
passion part of my life
when I belonged to you
and you belonged to me

Grief

once there was no time for laughter
and a distraught urgency for levity
became a simple smile or a chuckle
brief perhaps but uncommonly pure
as if adversity were a horizon line of grief
and sea met sky without protest
just a sigh in silence

the earth produced green shoots of laughter
enough to challenge silence
and blend into doubt's thunder

in the midst
voices subtle and endlessly different
continued

careening through space
often not bravely
hiding behind tears and fears
while lips remained smiling
for some semblance of sanity

The Path

alone

I started up the path
my thoughts a blank slate
and then I reached for his hand
reality a ghost

what I felt
uncertainty
rocks and gravel slippery
how could I move forward
without his strength
and when I looked back
I saw a precipice and gorge so deep
I could not fathom its finality

where was the hand
guidance
once taken for granted
without it I must still move
forward
looking back not an option
my path haunted by certain destruction
not one step to dare

then frozen here and now
frozen with fear
waning confidence dimming sunlight
and coating the stones
with slippery mist
my path emerged
a road a way forward
littered with pebbles of doubt

I knew
I knew with dread filling my being
I must move one foot
heavy almost paralyzed
and then the other
until pebbles and rocks became sand
and my path would lead
to places I might explore

alone

Autumn

September leaves
September sorrows
smiles of summer
still shining some mornings
and echoes
echoes of melodies
crashing waves
summer sands cooling
passions fading
mist hovering in moonlight
September songs
memories murmuring
promises
almost forgotten

Regret

did I tell him I loved him
of course I did
that's what I said

now that he's dead
and I'm not sure
just when or how
I said those words
why couldn't it be this day
when the feeling overflows my soul
and I know I will never be whole
again or feel the warmth of his sun
now that my **two** are only **one**

Loneliness

tree branches
scratch the slate of sky
silently

rain soaked earth
and descending clouds
join in reluctant embrace

memories drift
between twisted outlines
of winter's barren limbs

needles of rain
break bleak expanses
with their unexpected
glints of silver

at the top
of a leaf-bare branch
a bird's shadow
alone in maze of twigs
seeks an answering call

Solitude

whispering trees deceive me
for I cannot comprehend
their tender blessings
in a forest of uncertainty

why reach for Winter's solitude
and icicles of loss

barren limbs are brittle
no blood within their veins
they claw the sky
like ancient storms

I follow a deserted path
and imagine faint rustling
Spring is far away
and so is sorrow's birth

can I forget
or even want to
hearing the trees whisper
and taunt me
with their illusive location

p.m. – a.m.

that night was long
antiseptic
shadowed with futility
in unwelcoming arms
of an emergency area's
waiting room
sticky floors my tennis shoes protested
gum and half-filled candy wrappers
cola cans leaving
a thin amber trail
as they rolled over and over
on the linoleum
sounds sickening as the scents
low moans
hacking confusion
silent tears

time to wait
time to think

afterwards
still worried and at a loss for words
I walked slowly
into the deserted parking lot
just a rim of light
floated like a ghost
through the mist
velvet silence
in a motionless frame

as I drove
headlights began to wander
through the grayness
autos' shrill horns
and tires lapping the pavement
began to break the silence
and when I reached home
night had faded into dawn
the sky aglow with promise
of a bright clear day

Reflecting

the lamp is on
beside your bed
crumpled sheets
reflect dawn's sheen

faint scents of three a.m.
linger like ghosts of passion
unable to dissipate their hunger
while cold stars prick the sky
and lamplight wanders aimlessly
across empty folds

Voice of the Sea

the sea speaks to me in twilight
a red sun painting beach sands
my love and I sitting close
wrapped in a blanket of silence
savoring the drama of sky and surf
and echoes of waves caressing the shore

the sea speaks to me in noon's warmth
and laughter of my childhood
dancing in foam
building sand castles
shouting at breaking waves
watching sea life bubble up
through wet sand

the sea speaks to me in morning's tranquility
in mist during long walks along the shore
water lapping at my bare ankles
depression eased into fog

the sea speaks to me of strength and continuity
playful waves and serene waters
stretching toward virgin sands
tide moods changing suddenly
storms and clearing skies

Lost Lover

I couldn't imagine
this kind of loneliness before
emptiness that knows no filling
a need for touch
and whispered confidences

I can't imagine
following a strange path
a road unexplored
shrinking with sadness
an unresolved speck
not yet dust
and swept along

A Visit

we stand at his graveside
sunlight slanting
harsh emphasis
on a bronze engraving
we stand away from ourselves
polished statues
in the glare
son daughters wife
in silence

(Life's) Journey Through the Redwoods

we tried to find our way
that day and tripped through
vines and slippery leaves
and low stick-skeletons of branches
causing us pain

we looked up
surely a blue sky and blooming sun
would greet us
at least warm us as we struggled
through the underbrush
still the trees' branches
taller than most men could climb
clasped arms in a giant
canopy above us
a tent so large
only fragmented mirrors of light
shone through the fabric
and darkness competed
with the coming night

unable to swallow our fears
or risk a moment of rest
we continued our journey
made no conscious decisions
only held hands
embracing for mutual support
not noticing the Redwoods' grandeur

Serenity

I am where
loneliness has led me
into shadowed greenery

where birds have flown
leaving their nests abandoned
like afterthoughts

my branches bend and break
an old woman's figure
tired and drenched with solitude
and a winter storm

I am rooted to serenity
longing to experience it

Whispers

can you hear me
for my strength is gone
and all
that my meager breath
can manage
are whispers
that beseech you
to visit me

to sit for a while
next to me
so near
that I may feel
your warmth

I cannot cry out
in a whisper
and sobs are painful

if you turn
slightly
you will be able
to hear
the soft words
I utter
if you listen to me
you will know me
for these few minutes
and I will not
be lonely

Appointment

air around me
is heavy with mist
and difficult to breathe
disarray of clouds
in a dark sky
confuses my reality

upholstery is rough
against my skin
honking horns and tire skids
invade
my thoughts
offend my ears

I am not sure of the way
I can not
must not be late
my friend Jon
is being buried today

Unforgettable

photographs
cracked sepia
in aging anecdotes
point of view
unrecognized
background
invades edges
contours softened
definition blurred
features uncertain
fainter still
invisible

unforgettable

Coffee

I caress my coffee cup
it feels warm in my hands
like a comforting thought
like a gentle embrace

I sit alone in my den
viewing old family pictures
hung crookedly on plaster walls
and their off center stance
does not disturb me

I sip the warm brew
sugared simply sweetly
like memories
like pictures hung crookedly
on my den walls

later
the china cup begins to feel
cool in my grasp
and a hint of bitterness
is left in my cup
as I slowly taste my loses

The Box

somewhere
in a dark corner
surrounded by the musty smell
of many months
a box taped
with yellowing plastic
and covered with a gossamer web
of memories
its frayed edges
like an old novel
dusted with neglect

one day noticed
one day visible
and pulled into the sunlight
away from the anonymity
of my garage's crowded corner

I sit alone
not wanting
the reality of today an intrusion
as my gloved hands push away cobwebs
and wiping across years' debris
rip fragile cardboard
and open the box

I barely notice dust
floating around me
my hands tremble
as memories settle
around me and I wonder
what was fragile
enveloped in the scent of storage
what was treasured and preserved
resting in a cloud of tissue

slowly I touch each object
and hum an old tune
Is that all there is …
wondering why
those lyrics come to mind
while I carefully caress my treasures

Clay Dancer

the clay dancer
faces a mirror
and is poised to begin
a gift standing alone
feet on pointe
not of life
still life-like
turned towards her reflection

each birthday
I am greeted by a dancer

a porcelain ballerina
turning on a plate of music
a furry bear
dressed in satin and lace
huge feet stuffed
into pink toe shoes
an awkward doll
two feet high
with arms askew
gangly legs
green ballet slippers
and a purple net tutu

once a charcoal sketch
almost trashed
because of what
he considered imperfection
Queen of the Swans
arms extended head bowed

I wanted to be a ballerina
it was my passion
and he knew
recognized my dancer's dream
with tokens such as these
on my birthday
each year

Remembrance

my thoughts rippled into consciousness
only a toy
a toy in a glass hutch
incongruous among china cups
tarnished lusterless silver
dusty crystal
and chipped china plates
in the background
like friendly smiles
behind the clutter

just a little red truck
easily resting
in the palm of my hand
shiny metal with black wheels
and doors that opened
on miniature hinges

my tears were an ache
behind my eyes
as I remembered forty years later
a stormy April evening
windshield wipers clicking an accompaniment to
Bewitched, Bothered and Bewildered
sitting close to him in his big red truck
when his words crept out
I can't think of any reason
why we shouldn't get married …
so, how about it?

and then on our first anniversary
a red toy truck
on our dresser
next to a neatly printed note

How about another ride?

Changing Times

when times grow dark
I retreat into books
allow music to enter my soul
until my thoughts begin to clear
until I can open my eyes
and recognize pain
while the flow of tears
releases sadness

when times bring joy
I open each door and window
speak to the sun
dance in the wind
gain energy in its arms
laugh with the joy of it
paint my dreams on a mirror
and smile through the colors

Blossoms in the Sand

I sit here alone
my blanket laid out on the sand
my heart shrinking with profound grief
and I search for something
for an answer for comfort
for some kind of solution

now I look toward the sea
a sash of blue in the distance
small lines of foam
like chuckles at its edge
and I think about my place in the universe
about life and death inevitable as the tides

I sift warm sand through my fingers
and it almost feels alive
how does it nourish the sparse garden
of pink and magenta blossoms among thick jade leaves
twirling around debris and scattered
in clumps along the shore line

a whisper of breeze interrupts my thoughts
softens anguish so recently grown of despair
while the sea speaks to me
speaks of continuity of life
and reality of crashing waves
pulled back to sea like unfulfilled dreams

this moment is mine
sifted through my thoughts like the warm sand
and illusive blooms in the dusk
the sea's interlude of sighing tranquility
a cloudless sky fading through sunset
an interval of acceptance

sand around me begins to ripple
in a sudden gust
I am ready to go home now
I gather my blanket around me
wrapping myself in its warmth
and carefully pick a few blooms
holding them
like tender treasures against my breast
as I walk barefoot away from the sea

Night Winds

night winds surround me
embrace me with gentle arms of a lover
perfume my pillow with forgetfulness

within my troubled solitude
they make whisper sounds
in language strange and familiar

seeking comfort in solutions
I reach for diamond stars
their glittering perfection a dream

I fashion an intricate necklace
its glowing galaxy an illusion
flirting with me then slipping away

night winds whisper through my hair
laughing at the lost baubles
and perfume my pillow with tenderness

Falling Leaves

leaves strewn across my path
red and gold
brown and green
reminders
like whispers from my past
faded crumbling
some blazes of color
some hidden
glistening emerald

like paper birds
they float down
from ancient trees
blown with abandon
here and there
watered by tears of rain
within my thoughts

voices barely audible
I listen for love songs
and lonely clarinets
children chanting nursery rhymes
amidst the falling leaves

I listen for his chuckle
I listen for laughter
laughter brushing the sidewalk
laughter so illusive
I strive to recognize it
among the falling leaves

Awakening

a lone bird sings
outside my window
in the filmy hour
between night and dawn

a bird who warbles clearly
his tune guiding me
into wakefulness
in the reluctant hour
between night and dawn

my tired eyelids tremble
feeling warmth and a whisper of light
as I listen to melodic chirping
in the fading hour
between night and dawn

I have slept with pain and loss
searched my dreams for purpose
changed their form and fancy
followed their wistful wanderings
ushered them from reality
while an optimistic song
breaks through the silence
in the filmy hour
between night and dawn

Recovery

I stood alone,
in shivering reality
searching for protective arms
close enough to make their presence known
puzzle piece shadows
among barren branches
shaken by the same chill
that numbed my senses

now I stand aware of mountains
brushed with white paint
residing serenely
under a canopy of pink and purple silk
breezes stirring tranquil trees
thirsty at water's edge
and shaking off drifts of snow

I stand alone recovering
my eyes recently filled with emotion
cleared to reflect the landscape
I am at peace
alone and unafraid
in the wilderness of my thoughts

A Time to Laugh and A Time to Weep

her laughter
is a necklace of bells
and peals forth
with the spirit of a child
mesmerized by a bumble bee

her laughter ripples
like water in a mountain stream
rushing over rocks
and tumbling over itself
unable to stop

her laughter grows
from smiles to chuckles
from chuckles
to a clarion call
echoing across the years

her tears are dew-decorated petals
brushing across a face
lined with afterthoughts
her tears become mist so fine
they only blur the landscape

her tears are whispers
clinging to her eyelashes
and thin clouds
draping crooked shadows
across her cheek

her tears speak with silent voices
and combine until
they become an eddy of sorrow
that slowly swirls
toward the shadowed shore

Listen, Teacher

if only we would listen

to what our children say

Listen, Teacher

CONTENTS

Author's Note	108	Max	129
Listen, Teacher	109	Deana	130
Carpool	110	Armando	131
School Bells	111	Estella	132
Re-birth	112	Pedro	133
Teacher Cuts Class	113	Karyn	134
First Day	114	Tomas	135
Playground	115	A Conversation with Cindy	136
Danielle	116	Dora	138
Javier	117	Kathy	139
Maria	118	Bernice	140
Joey	119	Fidel	141
Twins	120	Billy	142
Frankie	121	Manuel	143
Mario	122	Molly	146
Nadine	123	Sheryl	147
Pamela	124	Daniel	148
Leonardo	125	Ginger	149
Delia	126	Do Not Break the Circle	150
Julie	127	First Grade Graduation	152
Gino	128	A Teacher Mourns	153

Author's Note

The children sketched in this book are a fictitious composite put together in a mosaic of memories and reactions I experienced during my many years as an elementary school teacher.

Listen, Teacher

If only we would listen
to what our children say
we'd be charmed …
our eyes would glisten,
as we learn from them each day.

A teacher's mantra in silent recognition:
I learn from my students,
about them and their world,
and also
about myself.

Carpool

we ride together each morning
for convenience
and to work as teachers
in the same school
children's voices echo
against traffic's hum
lesson plans jumble
and blur within our imagination
while fatigue and hope
struggle for recognition

the tears are not there
at 7:00 a.m. their urgency
dispelled by morning coffee
make-up covers our flaws
and our conversation streams
over the cracked glass of reality
too gently to shatter it

School Bells

ring ring ring
time for school to begin
paper pencils sniffles charts
sharing caring
phonics
talking chalk boards

recess time
out to play
a sunny day and drinks
bathroom time then
run fast away away
all the way
to the chain link fence
time for lunch
spaghetti and brownies
spilled milk and spilling tears

ring ring ring
time for home
glad days angry days
funny or sad
ready to leave

coats and sweaters
lunch boxes and
oh yes homework

Bye bye teach… bye, bye.
I love you!

Re-birth

the tree people
came to Morningside School
presenting sparse spikes
baby trees
cuddled in paper cones
nested in a spoonful of earth
sustenance

six inches of promise
fragile
boldly implying
importance

a pedigree of care
clutched by a Second Grader's hand
a living symbol
a quiet plea for life
possibility of growth
with nurturing

depending on inexperience
and enthusiastic care
for a future
showing faith in tomorrow
and a child's love

Teacher Cuts Class

I snip black paper
curves here straight edges there
her rounded brow whisper of lash
nose long and delicate
his chin somewhat square
and far above hair
curled and swirled
over a proud forehead
and feathered down his neck

I snip black paper
and look once again
at Eugenia and Francisco
the flat black pictures
ARE my young students
sculpted to their likeness
because I know and love these children

I snip black paper
and think about the life the shine
that cannot be revealed
in the silhouettes
I so diligently create
portraits ready to be pasted
on virgin white paper
and sent home for Christmas

First Day

I'm new in school, are you?
(My shoes are old and tight …
too tight and the wrong color.
I wanted purple … purple shoes
to match my socks
and I'm new.
I didn't want them black!)

I'm new in school too.
(But my dress isn't new.
It's long and wrong,
not right, mama!
And I'm new
and the dress isn't blue.
Are you wearing the wrong dress too?)

I'm new in school. Are you?
(My stomach hurts.
My ears itch.
My hands are sweaty
and too big and I have
no pockets to put them in.
Why mama, didn't you think of pockets?)

I'm new in school. Are you?
(Something is choking me
and not letting go!
Do you know? I'm new! I'm new!
I don't know what to do
or where the bathrooms are
or how I get a star.)

When can I go?
Let me know! Let me know!

Playground

Down by the river,
Down by the sea,
Johnny broke a bottle
And blamed it onto me!
snap hop snap hop
turn turn and turn again
up and down and around
I sit in the shade
near the gritty sand box
and idly hold my whistle
listening to the screams and sobs
to the sing-song chants
to the hopping rhythm of sandals
scraping asphalt

and I wonder as I watch my children
hands embrace
hands push away
hands throw sand
or slap in anger
someone is alone
and always sad
sometimes someone is glad
at recess time

over there three or four
arms entwined
voices chanting smiling faces
impish giggles
over there taunts and screams
Unfair, unfair!
and I sit in the shade
near the gritty sand box
waiting for the bell

Danielle

Why don't they like me?
you asked that day
and what could I say
as I watched you play
alone with the blocks
alone with the jacks
turning toward
their turned around backs

taking a breath
you're unable to shout
they're running and laughing
and no one's about

Javier

his pencils talk
his crayons speak in intensities
color and contrast

the cannon rips yellow and red
flaming into the bogus
and showers bits of light

his face beams shyly
behind the exploding stars
as he squints to view his work
Is it the bestest? Javier asks

accept what they say the way they say it
It certainly is!

Javier on welfare with really gold capped teeth
I wish I could take
his gentle smile home with me

Maria

come with me, Maria
don't be afraid
I'll hold your hand
I'll understand
it's you and I
we are together
for now at least

your timid hand
can't squeeze hard enough
to hurt me
and you don't mind
your arm stretching high
to meet mine

Joey

one pointed tooth is a grin
how did it get that way
I couldn't say
but Joey knows
and his smile says
I'm great you know!

off he runs
animal grace
makes the boy a man
makes no mistake
and the grin is there
even when I can't see
his face

Twins

Debra and Donna
delight me
with their identical
green and brown flecked eyes
and missing teeth grins
sometimes my confusion
delights them
as they peek out
from under their
Buster Brown bangs
and hide their giggles
behind tiny fingers
nails decorated
with chipped red polish
and I'm not quite sure
who is who

so small
they might appear to be
four instead of seven
rounded plump
wearing ruffled dresses
the same wide white collars
and puffy sleeves
hand in hand
they are almost one
just a whisper apart
a skip a beat
in another direction
a tentative smile
a new friend
tears shed alone
laughter not echoed

Frankie

oh Frankie dear Frankie
why do you cry
sobs torn from you
by wounds too deep
for me to understand

tears
rivulets on your cheeks
silver streams like rain
flowing down a window pane

your moans
are a lost bird
calling for help
too softly
much too softly to be heard
after the shrill sobs
have disappeared

Mario

your paint brushes are magical
they fly over paper
like bright birds
wings brushing colors
purple yellow blue red
bright green
vibrant pictures
your expression colorless
while your painting shouts
with joy in its creation

Nadine

fetal position again
against what

would you like
to join our circle
sing a song
feed the guinea pig

will you trust my smile
for just a little while
are you ready to listen
while I strum the autoharp
Frere Jacques Frere Jacques

I want to take you
in my arms
and make your world
all better

Pamela

stay this wintry day
and spin a tale
tell a story
words and pictures
and smiles of childhood

comb your hair
in the wind
let it fly about
do not be blinded
by strands across your eyes
or words scattered on paper

wonder caressing you now
brushed away
like petals of no value
falling at your feet
and crushed unnoticed

Leonardo

I have a beau
a first grade beau
with jam-smeared face
and seven hundred and forty five freckles

I have a beau
who never stops
talking or skipping
or jumping about

I have a beau
with green cat's eyes
a Spanish accent
and yellow hair

I have a beau
who brings me bananas
unwrapped sugar cubes
and a single earring for Christmas

I have a beau
who writes backwards
and can't add or subtract
but paints fantastic clowns

I have a beau
who loves me
though I scold him
and insists on holding my hand

Delia

a cross resides proudly
on her plump young chest
she wears hoop earrings
red ribbons in her hair
and a patient smile

three brothers and a sister
are younger than six
Delia tends to them
with mama and washes
all the dishes at home

Delia can read
and change a diaper
Delia can print a story
and burp a baby
Delia can add and subtract
and buy groceries by herself

Delia can recite verse
put her sister to bed
and get her brother
to school every day
and never be late
Delia is never tardy

Julie

Jumping Jack Julie
pops up and down
hands waving for recognition
feet racing to be first

Julie jumps up
to catch a ball first
or catch on to an idea
tossed high above her head

her brown braids
bounce in rhythm
to sticks dancing on drums
while her feet tap in time

Julie a child quick to respond
quick to laugh or cry
and explode from her box
like an animated toy

Gino

high cheekbones
crimsoned
with sun and rubbing
fringed
by thick black lashes

eyes white and black
glinting squinting
avoiding
pain or purpose

hair straight and stiff
carefully groomed
up up
from a high forehead

his smile unsure or absent
not showing teeth
the sculpture of his cheek
only slightly changed

arms and legs muscular
strong extensions
from a lean body
in army fatigues

Gino leads the line
not looking back
a soldier marching
unquestioning

Max

your wild eyes
may be a disguise
still there is something there
in the terror of your stare
in your shoulders hunched
in fear of what
your hand over your pocket
over the pocket knife
over the strife
over the rebukes and slaps

look this way Max
past their taunts
do not lose yourself
there in confusion
yours is a cruel world
outside and in
I can't read! I can't read!
your eyes swim with tears and loss

you toss your head
and bang it on the desk
Don't leave it there!
Sit up! Sit up!
someone is here for you
the rest are not
and that is what you've got

*D*eana

a dimpled darling
Deanna loves to sing
La La La La La

instead of
This Land is Your Land
this land is her land
a small bird
with a twinkling voice
while I strum
my autoharp
From California to the New York Island
La La La La La

Armando

those tennis shoes
are too tight
still nice and new
it hurts for him
to walk in them
no matter he is proud

his jeans are torn
and his zipper stuck
what does he do
those twenty trips to the bathroom
before noon

today he shared
up in front of the whole class
someone gave him a Ninja toy
he spoke through missing teeth
we couldn't understand a single word

Thank you Armando !

Estella

Estella is my secretary
she wears a paper badge
declaring her position

her lips are pursed
her head bent over her work
while she
counts milk money
folds copy sheets
gets paper and pencils ready

she wanders from desk to desk
busily passing out supplies
and listens for the office buzzer
ready to be a messenger

her gold flecked brown eyes
speak to me
focused serious
waiting for me to start the day
a signal for her to do her job

like a baby bird
beginning to fly
she hovers near me
prettily poised
a box of blue pencils in her hands

Estella doesn't speak a word of English

Pedro

once Pedro brought a pet to school
sharing time how sublime
to bring a pet lizard
and charm the class

alarm the creature escaped
whipped away across the floor
to screams of delight at the sight
and disappeared
I knew not where
I was up on a chair

chaos and laughter
Pedro in tears
my worst fears

the pet never found
a sad fact
still my nerves left in tact

dear dear Pedro dry your tears
the years will heal your loss
and your lucky lizard is free at last

Karyn

you are your own puppeteer
and you pull the strings deftly
your ribbons are bright and new
every day they adorn a different hairdo
and make rainbow sashes

you are always first
the leader of the line
because you pull the strings
and all the other little ones
are afraid they'll get tangled up

you smile down you frown up
you interrupt and pout
still you are a winner a blue-eyed winner
in Alice in Wonderland gowns
and patent leather shoes

no one has ever said
your defect made a difference
in fact
no one has ever noticed it
and your arrogance hides your pain

Tomas

Tomas the scientist
I watch you watch
the butterfly wings
emerging
wet
sticky
beating
now in that little glass cage
magic happens
you observe with glee

for what you see prompts you
to clap your hands
your eyes filled with wonder
your mind eager to explore

A Conversation with Cindy

Daddy hit me hard.
Why?
Well, that man cut my hair.
What man?
You, know. The man who comes over lots
of times to see my mommy and bring me
bubble gum.
Your daddy was angry about your hair?
Yeah, boy was he ever! He really yelled!
And what did your mom do?
Oh, nothin'. She said she didn't care.
Didn't care that you got hit?
No, didn't care that my hair got cut.
Anyways, I got new socks.
Some lady went and got me socks.
Oh! A friend?

No, some lady that was all dressed up. I
don't know her.

She came to see mommy and gave me socks.

Wasn't that nice?

Nope!

Nope?

They itch!

Oh ....

And pretty soon Daddy's comin' home for
good and we're goin' to Marineland and
Disneyland and the zoo like we used to and
my socks won't itch.

Oh!

Teacher?

Yes?

Do your socks itch?

Dora

silken hair
sheltering black wing
covers half her face
and glides across her shoulders

Dora's words
shyly spoken
like a dove's soft call
from a high branch

her shadow dances
behind her
in the middle
of the class line
where no one notices
her voice is lost
amidst the chatter

Kathy

trickle of bangs
and trickle of tears
I won't ! I won't ! I won't !
then
I can't !

how could I know

oh yes she can read
she can sing and dance and scream
add two columns
pinch and jab
a blue pencil through paper

tear it up up up
confetti in the air

I was so sure everything was all right
so sure the bits of paper
could be swept up

Bernice

within an amber orb
pupil ignited by inner fire
widens its dimension
spirit unable to escape

laughter resounds
echoes in my ear
joy not conscious of self
head thrown back awkwardly

wide smile set in a narrow profile
Bernice grasps sparkling gifts
hugging treasures to her breast
excitement out of control

suddenly wrenching sobs
inevitably retreat to Teacher
pearls trembling manicured nails blinking
against her blue silk jumper

Fidel

Fidel's smile
is wide and constant
a grin often punctuated by laughter
he hugs himself with joy
singing loudly and off key
his hearing aids are clearly visible
and he shows them off proudly

fresh faced funny eager loving
Fidel is an A plus student

Billy

Billy loves to play ball
bounce it bat it kick it
all the same

his sneakers race
with swiftness of their own
and his jeans fit tightly
their frayed cuffs
sweep the asphalt
as he runs runs runs
just behind the bouncing ball
he is about to capture

Manuel

one gray day
or was it sunny
I don't recall at all
still that day remains
a memory keeper
it was the time I lost
young Manuel on a field trip

Line up everyone.
my voice was urgent
our big school bus
black and yellow bumble bee
arrived on time
motor buzzing impatiently

Thirty-two Thirty-three Thirty-four
young Manuel the last
holding my aide's hand tightly
All aboard!
our destination Lake Hollywood

a sparking jewel a reservoir
nestled in the Hollywood hills
unexpected sight surrounded by greenery
reflecting giant oaks pines
and wild walnut trees

too deep too far
two billion gallons of danger
some places paths had no fences
I shouted warnings to my aide
and my children
Listen to directions!

eager children held hands
with partners sharing hushed delight
faces painted with awe
at the shimmering mirror
and grand and whispering trees
woodpeckers humming birds blue jays
cavorting among branches

wide-eyed and wondering students
their line like a rippling ribbon
circled the silver reservoir
and hummed with subdued enthusiasm

when it was time to leave
the tired children lined up quietly
ready to go home
Thirty-two Thirty-three...
suddenly my aide called out in despair
young Manuel had wandered off

my heart stopped beating
then thundered in my chest
far in the distance
in a danger zone close to the water
young Manuel strolled unaware
of the impatient bus
or children slowly boarding

I stood calmly waiting
afraid to move
afraid to become part of
Manuel's Hide and Seek game

his small figure
yards and yards away
strolled slowly towards me
oblivious to the danger
a stray bird coming to roost
with a shy smile
he reached for my hand

safe

Molly

like a moth to light
she reaches for a book
and flutters through the pages
with abandonment and joy

Molly makes friends
with Rapunzel and Snow White
cavorts among the Seven Dwarfs
becomes entangled in Charlotte's Web

like a moth she flutters
from page to page
alights momentarily on a picture
flies over each story
comes to rest wings spread

Sheryl

welcome to Morningside
my new student Sheryl
wearing a bright yellow slicker
and black galoshes

you splash in the rain
like a big golden butterfly
flitting from friend to friend
then cling to my hand
trembling with energy
ready to line up for class

Sheryl loves the rain
her smile is a rainbow

Daniel

shock of red hair
freckles everywhere
his ready smile greets me
with the morning bell
and flickers from eight to three

meanwhile Daniel dawdles and doodles
marking on every scrap of paper
on the front
on the back
on each corner
between spelling words
next to number columns
oblivious to the big school clock
making warning faces at him

some days among the doodles
between the squiggles lines and circles
like a small flower in a garden of weeds
a unique picture emerges
and I smile as I paste a big gold star next to it

Ginger

Ginger's face is the color
of desert sands
her hair a flaming sunset

she dances in and out
of room 15
music somewhere within her
accompanied by laughter
and her patent leather shoes
tapping along hallways

she always wears a costume
white dresses adorned with flowers
a red rose
clipped in her hair
quivering in time
to her own music

Do Not Break the Circle

this must not happen
not on my watch
not among citizens
in my first grade classroom

young voices harsh threatening
You can't play with us,
stay away from us,
you stink you're ugly,
you're a baby, a scaredy cat.
I'll beat you up after school!
pictures and words on bathroom walls
red paint inflicted on gray

no way I say
what can I do
eyes in the back of my head
cannot see all
I watch what I can
hear what I can
drift among the children
in my classroom community
and do what I can

stop don't how can you
I won't let you
my heart demands
like an irate mother
still I am a teacher
I studied psychology and sociology
how can I heal the human spirit
when I am so often defeated
helpless among attacking shadows

watch carefully
find clues
when were the seeds
of anger and cruelty planted
in what tainted soil did they grow
how can hostility be tamed
its energy fly like a bright kite
In a peaceful sky

wounds must not be inflicted
they will **not** happen on my watch
give each child a crown of self-esteem
athlete artist tutor monitor
stars and awards

join a circle hold hands
sing together share stories
form a bond of trust
talk talk talk
words about feelings
do not break the circle
warm hands held tightly
tears may fall
do not break the circle
angry words may float about
hold hands tightly
talk about injuries
why why why

do not break the circle
before my six-year-olds
grow to be twelve
and their wounds
are too deep to heal

First Grade Graduation

my young students stand before me
children I have come to know and love
I have wiped their tears
comforted them inspired them
honored their uniqueness
guided them at the beginning
of their perilous path to adulthood

twelve years from now
they will face
a constantly changing world

will they be adept enough
to master and adjust
will they find a way
to survive
the uncertain days
will they be strong enough
to carry others in need
will the sun continue to shine upon them
and the atmosphere protect them
will laughter and joy
maintain their souls
creativity nourish their minds
and will some innocence remain

will I be here
to see them as adults
and still recognize their faces

A Teacher Mourns

I looked up at a changing sky
lights and darks
like a charcoal sketch
a sky covered by a cloak of mystery
torn by slivers of silver
swept away in tattered wisps

dusk slowly approached
the sun low behind me
when a giant rainbow suddenly emerged
colors defined in a sparkling prism
red orange yellow green blue violet
an arch quivering in the rain drenched canopy

I stood alone shivering in late afternoon chill
and felt mist tears on my cheek
my heart throbbed and tears became a sob
for a long time I contemplated the tenacious image
my hands frozen in prayer

when I suddenly became aware
realized
finally understood
felt with a certainty beyond reason or logic
twenty small angels had painted
that arch of wonder

and I remember my own first graders
standing by easels
their colorful paint-smeared aprons
and joyfully splashed papers
as they painted rainbows

In memory of SandyHook tragedy
Newtown, Connecticut 12/14/12

CHAPTER IV

Dancin'

those who dance are fireflies

sometimes mistaken for stars

CHAPTER IV

Dancin'

CONTENTS

Invitation 159

Those Who Dance 160

Join the Circle. 162

Partners 163

Tango 164

By the Flaming Lake 165

Musical Notes in My Life. 166

Dress Rehearsal 167

Folk Dancers' Celebration 168

Dancing in the Shadows 169

Chronicle of a Clarinet 170

Can We Still Dance? 172

Steps in Time 173

My Dancing Shoes Trilogy 174

Invitation

music begins
strange instruments and rhythms
folk songs and melodies
beckoning to the dancers

sometimes in groups
sometimes alone
we drift into a circle
as if led by a Pied Piper
into steps of the dance

musical notes become part of me
and I am one with the others
ache in my muscles
is forgotten
sadness in my heart
slowly fades
while I quicken to the melody

warmth of hands I hold
eases me
smiles surrounding me
are a gift
doors of grief and pain close
and music
echoes back from them
as the circle I am part of
draws closer

Those Who Dance

those who dance
find the earth covered
by uncertain clouds too illusive
to support heavy steps

mold the mist
into moving shadows
listen to musical leaves
hold waving branch arms
like partners in the wind

lie on beach sands
lifted by changing tides
ripple upon ripple
gently urging them
to join the waves
and float into center
of sea circles

those who dance
twirl in and out of reality
become lost in games
books and deep thoughts
don costumes
drift into a fading sunset
with the others
like wisps of clouds

those who dance
know the seasons
become part of them
understand ripples
a stone can make
in a lake of reason

become reflections
chandelier lights on night walls
petals falling from a rose
harp strings children's smiles

those who dance sing
for how can they not
when their voices also dance

those who dance
are not afraid to cry
their spirits do not drown in tears
only bend with the wind
they remain resolute
and fall asleep in the arms
of a melody

those who dance are fireflies
flitting in a warm spring night
sometimes mistaken for

stars

Join the Circle

dancin' around
on toe and heel
summer nights Saturday or Sunday
any time the music plays
no tapping foot is able to resist

why not dance on starless nights
and twirl my skirts
and clap in time

the band plays
hidden figures
among rustling leaves
and calling birds

I'll join the circle
remain in shadows
or trip along a garden path
and feel wet grass
clinging to my bare feet

Partners

in dance competition
you two are
a winning pair

you have rhythm and balance
listen to music's subtleties
and move with grace

you are beautifully matched
retain your individuality
remain in harmony
and interpret the melody
reflecting its beauty
even when strident chords echo

Tango

night's arms
embrace dancers
and the Tango begins
music pulsing with
their heartbeats
imprisoned personalities

twist of her leg
locked to his
by a pointed patent pump
swish of silk
and black lace caressing
cold alabaster limbs

an arrogant rose
attached to her polished helmet
brittle chignon
motionless
in the syncopated rhythm

expressionless austerity dances
with haunting authority
personality struggling to be free
still imprisoned
by the violin's strings

By the Flaming Lake

night shadows close in
softening flames of sunset
while sky colors fade

will you dance with me
here by the flaming lake
along slippery rocks
I will hold your hand
and leap-step away from the waters
into a meadow's cool greenery

a lake stained by sunset
my naked figure reflected in restless waters
the pool's lines of rebellion
vibrant in stillness
my life tangled in underbrush
an abyss of uncertainty

where are the fireflies
their lights danced
away in twilight

Musical Notes in My Life

Mozart and Bach
greeting the dawn
counter-point a new day

Tchaikovsky blaring forth
through my car radio
erases traffic demons

autoharp's twang
children's rhyming songs
hot muggy teaching days

Glen Miller and Les Brown
nostalgia in a clarinet
college dances in San Francisco

Scottish tunes and fiddlers
sets of eight assembled
patterns changing to the beat

Swan Lake's graceful dancers
Sunday night's special date
ballet performance at the Shrine

Bewitched Bothered and Bewildered
a rainy afternoon at the beach
and a romantic proposal

Old McDonald and *Brother John*
grandchildren sing off key
on a bumpy ride home

Dress Rehearsal

dearest mom how many hours
did you search for patterns and fabric
sewn with your head bent low in dim light
rhythm of the Singer lulled me to sleep
then in quiet mysterious dawn
I found each costume hung in my closet
enchantment decorating my life and dreams

you cut and sewed and hand-stitched
like an artist with your scissors and needle
creating a peach and gold lame tap tunic
George Washington's pantaloons and vest
a silken Japanese kimono
beribboned Gypsy skirts
an ice-blue satin and tulle tutu
magical memories all

my dear mother with your quiet ways
soft spoken at lessons and rehearsals
designing costumes of exquisite beauty
with no expectation of praise
your glow
in the thrill of creating

Folk Dancers' Celebration

seventy smiling faces
and many of us are at least seventy
every inch alive with music
twinges of regret and circumstance
vibrancy within each worn and weathered guest
dances in celebration
while seventy colored lights twinkle
in fading reality of twilight

our star studded future is all too uncertain
within encircling arms songs and dancing
and temptations of a bountiful table
we cannot always see smiles or hear laughter
they flow like vintage wine
over the cobblestones of our history

seventy smiling faces smoothed over
in a misty evening's balm
sometimes our voices become one
as we shuffle into quick steps
and race toward an early dawn

seventy golden rings intertwine
and glint bravely in dew-filled nights
with a pulse yearning for each broken link
remembering each embrace and steaming dish
remembering footsteps dance steps
twirling skirts and shiny boots
dancing in a broken circle
and darkened corridors of grief

still this night bursts with energy and resolve
with nostalgia by design
its pattern defined by necklaces of jingling coins
as optimistic as seventy smiles

Dancing in the Shadows

scarves flying
Yasous! echo
a mosaic of dancing figures
disappears between
shafts of light and dark

they re-appear singing
thin voices like violin strings
compete with chirping crickets
and I strain to hear them

skirts ripple
crimson yellow blue
flowers not quite visible
among wild blooms
and restless leaves

flirting figures
I struggle to recognize
sometimes I sense their presence
hidden in greenery
among twisted branches
and mists of yesterday

their footsteps
are formed of silence
as they dance over
fallen leaves
and soft supple earth

music is there
embracing them with joy
rhythms I remember
I hear them clearly
and they are part of the silence
circles of memories
twirling figures
my friends are dancing in the shadows

Chronicle of a Clarinet

musical notes imprinted
like coins of silver
on black ebony
a clarion voice yet to be heard

section by section
out of a red velvet box
one day put together
like pieces of a puzzle

a dusty store's mosaic of instruments
rentals and purchases
clarinets and piccolos
and a wide-eyed boy

a silent symphony
violins drums and clarinets
and printed sheets singing notes
to a wide-eyed and wondering boy

a price a purchase a treasure
a promise a future a friend
all held tightly in the hands
of an awkward and wide-eyed boy

and then
silver sonnets unsung
mouth pieces and reeds
agony of squeaks
painful in the midst
of clear and counted measures
and ragged breaths
fingers dancing
over a silver buttoned keyboard
the joy of a wide eyed boy

and then
polished with pride and singing
with ten clarinets
and ten drums
marching around Poly's field
mellow notes' perfection
caressing sounds and trumpets calling
youths like toy soldiers in perfect harmony
the tallest one a wide-eyed boy

and then
no voice no measured breath
no music past his lips
a dulled silver and ebony clarinet
packed into a worn red velvet case
a cherished dream
reluctantly surrendered to the past
by a wide-eyed youth

and then
friend to friend
a gift given
carefully reassembled to life
in glittering perfection
a soldier in an Army Band
notes swelling across the sea
still singing
realizing a life of its own
while a wide-eyed man remembers

Can We Still Dance?

can we still dance
with abandonment and joy
will our bodies
still supple
capture the rhythm and mood
are we too close
to winter's restraint
memories raining down
from hovering clouds

can I make you dance
pull your puppet strings
twirl you away
from darkness
into the violin and clarinet's
welcoming arms
into a moment of pure joy

Steps in Time

soft rock
one two one two
footsteps on sidewalks
exactly on the beat

staccato heels
click on cement
a secretary's sleek suit
and polished smile

heavy boots
no echo on each count
construction worker's
deliberate steps in time

lovers' waltz
gliding on rain mirrors
caressing the walkway
feet barely touching

children's arms swing
oblivious skipping
small sneakers
stub toes in cracks

steps of age
shuffling with lost grace
far behind
faint brushes on brass cymbals

My Dancing Shoes Trilogy

once I wore high heels
and waltzed under a glittering mirror ball
that showered silver coins
like giant raindrops
all around me
my feet floated
across the floor barely touching
its polished surface
I danced with a stranger
who held me within his stiff frame
while I melted into the music

☙

once I wore black leather sandals
and danced the Hasapico
in a Greek restaurant open
to Santa Monica breezes
musicians played the oud and clarino
while we danced with abandon

like children at a fair
a ribbon of dancers
weaving in between the tables
and saluted by patrons' OPAS!
Zorba's calls echoing down the line
wine laughter dancing
until everyone else had disappeared
and we toasted the dawn

☙

once I wore laced-up gillies
and a plaid scarf across my shoulder
bagpipes started our performance
Scottish dancers changing roles
in sets of eight
long ago tales translated
by strathspeys and jigs
into complicated patterns
and I was part of the puzzle
reels and pas de basques
bagpipes fiddles drums
pointed toes and kilts bouncing
polite greetings whenever
dancers met
patterns completed
each couple in turn
bagpipes sighed fiddles faded
drumbeats echoed away
while I waited for the next dance

CHAPTER V

Streets Scene

I cannot find my home
back and forth I wander
on the street where I lived

CHAPTER V

Streets Scene

CONTENTS

Field Trip to Watts Towers...... 181

Watts Towers of Triumph 182

Echoes 185

My Own Towers in Pacoima..... 186

Labor Force................ 187

Los Angeles Skyscraper........ 188

What Do I Know 189

Ghosts 192

Christmas Sale 195

Notes on a Metro Subway Tour .. 196

Los Angeles Theater, Downtown. 200

On the Street Where I Lived 202

Visiting Skirball Museum 204

Frozen in Time 206

Lincoln's Statue, Washington DC. 207

Pause in the Pageantry........ 208

Beacon on Coast Highway...... 209

No One Wears Tennis Shoes
   in Boston 210

Rose Avenue
   Venice Beach 1935.......... 212

Field Trip to Watts Towers

we met last week Simon
on a raw and sunny day
amidst shacks tattooed with iron bars
and cracked sidewalks
blackend by boots and roller-blades

we met within your home
you waved from the highest tower
threw your sweat-brimmed hat
into the air
and laughed at the wind

Watts Towers of Triumph

wonders of wizardry
one man's
monumental masterpiece
proud city
built of towers
pipes girded
with wire mesh
incongruous
among its neighbors
still at home
unafraid with
lopsided smiles
and bones of steel

barred entrances
hints of light
hints of life
behind the slats
this prism city
its mirrors just
shards of glass
looks down upon
huts of humiliation
tethered
by black bars
of fear
and frustration

among the towers
a chapel of stone
and serenity
its ceiling open
welcoming the star
filled night
within its dusty crevices
a liturgy composed of
broken glass
broken lives
mended with mortar

old news headlines
of hope
imprinted into
awkward church walls

lopsided towers
each one climbed
painfully
dangerously
daringly
to add one more
embellishment
one element closer
to the sun
twisted tendrils
of steel
balancing in
silhouette against
a fading sky

the towers
never fall
they stand stubbornly
a city glued
together of relics
dishes and dolls
beer bottles
glass the colors
of the sea
stones
pottery and porcelain
and jewelry
tears torment
history
of South Central L.A.
surviving earthquakes riots
neglect
arrogance of downtown's
edifices of progress
greed
and abandonment by
their maker

Echoes

winds blow through
the open structure
where Simon made friends
with the sky and the earth
and the dangerous streets

echoes long ago impressions
when I walked through
beautiful rubble without fear

sorry amber beer bottles
braided into the fabric of
a twisted metal chapel
in South-Central L.A.

remembering as winds blow
through my thoughts
I wrote a poem then

and another one now
a poem about
my own towers in Pacoima

My Own Towers in Pacoima

my towers toppled once
like dominoes one upon the other
it does not matter now
they were once built with strength
and their own unique beauty
like castles in a fairy tale

mortar mixed of laughter and cake flour
handmade organdy curtains
and a nursery with linoleum
alphabet squares

books and baby bottles and T-squares
and a player piano
boxes and boxes of pictures
turning yellow and crumbling

I remember only a framework
only green shag tripping my high heels
only hours soaking in bubbles
only hours listening
for his heartbeat muffled
in sheets and blankets

my towers built into dreams
my epitaph will read
She was a nice person
who found it difficult to cry.

Labor Force

Kester Street, Van Nuys, California 6:30 a.m. 2006

on concrete corners still damp
they greet an early dawn
there in morning chill
they search the mist

protected by threadbare sweatshirts
and duck-billed caps
some printed Dos Equis
a cigarette stub
shared among strangers
and smoke inhaled
bring small comfort

some sit on cracked curbs
defeat in their eyes
rough hands holding
the reality of tool boxes
wrinkled jeans
sneakers tied tightly
and cheap wristwatches taunt
as sunlight burns
through the paper sky

a car stops
window rolled down halfway
brief negotiations
and one is gone
his tool box forgotten
in haste
lies unnoticed
while strong men drift away
like dried leaves
along the sidewalk

Los Angeles Skyscraper

glass collects sunshine
and sparkles painfully
rows and rows
of perfect windows
hide imperfect decisions
justified behind them

framework of steel
cold in its certainty
with no possibility of compromise
competitive in height and geometry
challenges the sky
with its concrete reality

What Do I Know

gray cement banks of the L.A. River
unfeeling vessel
stained with blood of gang values
red and black silver and green
metallic sprays
wrestling for attention
sometimes scrubbed off
but never completely
how many times
how many times
with artistry
calligraphic masterpieces
design space and imagination
a painter's palette of invented colors
sprayed with precision
hidden artists climbing over barriers
night covering their tracks
like a giant eraser

what do I know
with my spectacles and first grade classroom
death looms like a monster to me
unacceptable in my everyday world
grief a long time healing

as I gaze through
a smudged train window
spray painted messages taunt death
invite it like a party guest
cheapen it to an initiation fee

what do I know
I haven't tasted hopelessness
or fear or failure much
and death is mourning too much to bear
giant block letters
symbols turned like acrobats
and competing for space or recognition
gang sounds and messages
alive and growling at the trains
roaring out of L.A.'s downtown station

what do I hear
beyond the drumbeat of wheels
playing on metal tracks
sounds are muffled as I pass
a mosaic of misery
thickened by layer upon layer of spray
eating the base of power poles
dripping down to water's edge
surrounding drainage hole homeless shelters
like cheap necklaces

what do I know
sitting by a smudged window to the world
seeing someone's laundry spread
over a cement canvas of graffiti

I whirl into a zone
of garish color and calligraphy
my train is going fast a tumultuous giant
when I suddenly hear the pleas
Don't paint over our voices…
we'll keep shouting anyway!
We are here
We are a fact!

maniacal masterpieces
giant block letters tumbling over each other
or fit together
like pieces of a puzzle

my printing is formed
First Grade perfect soldier straight lines
and clown-face circles
my initials stand for something
symbols mean something

if I were to emblazon my name
where would it fit
who would understand
what I stand for

what do I know
I don't own a spray paint can
and I can't see well in the dark

Ghosts

(A companion piece to What Do I Know)

my train leaves L.A. station
alive with the hum of commuters
smug in its speed and efficiency
a new train with clean windows
clear glass to view the outside world

water flows in the L.A. River bed
a foot of muddy litter-laced water
the color of sadness and defeat
too murky to reflect a cloud filled sky
while a few drops still prick the stream

drainage holes provide no access now
and I wonder where they are
those who once left their laundry and ragged tents
out to dry on garishly painted river banks
are they ghosts wandering and wondering
invisible from my train window
and shivering in murky regions

someone came along with giant rollers
and painted over the violent masterpieces
miles and miles of beige and white squares
hundreds of splashing buckets and hissing hoses
erasing garish graffiti with pristine paint
in some places a mosaic of stones
plastered against concrete riverbed walls
defying any invasion of paint or color
or feuding cries of anger

I don't see the ghosts or their symbols
their calligraphy obliterated
by dismal squares of nothingness
alternative to messages of vindictive violence
everything so clean so vulnerable so peaceful
still I know ghosts are there and coming back
I sense their presence
I see their shadows long and menacing across the concrete
and they have started to leave their mark again
in impossible places
under freeway bridges' eaves
colors laughing with scorn

giant three foot letters
just above the river's water line
boldly strutting their importance
faint outlines bleeding through the beige and white
like forgotten curses
I can't hear the shouts
ghosts have no voices
their spray paint cans are out there somewhere
unafraid hiding in moonless nights

my train is late traveling fast making up time
now unexpected glimpses
of graffiti art and words
begin to shout into the rumble of trains
they are trying to form a statement
large and bold and in outline
ready to burst into anger
images rush by me blended as though
viewed through a kaleidoscope
robbed of their messages but not their color
where squares of beige and white are interrupted

illusive ghosts are there all around us
invisible to most of us
those who carry their spray cans
and homeless ones lost and desperate
wandering into shelters
where food is too rich
and danger lurks in dark corners
ghosts looking for enemy ghosts
finally turn on themselves
while pitiful laundry floats down the L.A. River

the graffiti will return
I'm not sure about the laundry

Christmas Sale

mud colored houses
like frogs
on winter faded
grass ponds
in a solemn suburb
shed tears of isolation
through closed shutters

houses surrounded
by fence sheltered yards
scrubby bushes whispering
voices lost in the chill

I will string Christmas lights
red and green
blue and white
watch them blink loudly
against the dawn

tis the season here
somewhere everywhere
and for my pale blue
recalcitrant cottage
its voice muted
for it doesn't belong

now I am ready to paint
over my summer vision
mud colored paint
brushes full dripping
over the faded blue plaster

this holiday season
the realtors will
sharpen their pencils
like miniature scalpels
and smile in anticipation

Notes on a Metro Subway Tour

I enter a tube in a tunnel
guided by blinking neon signs
and settle into Metro's narrow car
strangers crowding into my space
their faces blank pages

a surprising lurch and we are off
acceleration propels me
forward in my narrow place
when suddenly lights appear
and invade the darkness

as we approach each station
a blur of street names and numbers
taunts me with brief moments of clarity
just coming into focus
through thick glass train windows

doors snap open with split second precision
forcing exit for most their destination
then snap shut and speed pulls us along
into a dark cave with blurred walls
I feel threatened and a desire to escape

I hold on to a slippery silver pole
and sway with the rhythm of the car
an awkward dancer alone with my thoughts
while a young father holds my pole briefly
a wiggly girl child clinging to his leg

strangers a chubby baby girl and a child-man
wearing a torn undershirt and wrinkled blazer

heading for Hollywood's opulent station
they debark
a trail of milk tears
dripping from the baby's bottle

doors snap open and I stumble out
breathless from my quick exit
suddenly blinded and alone
I am in a giant hall blasted by light
while school children follow a nun and sing
their sweet voices floating toward me
then I look up and see
thousands of empty movie reels
and my gaze is drawn toward the ceiling
toward a canopy of empty reels
naked in their loss and imprisoned
forever in a Metro station

I hold the hand rail and climb steep stairs
forgetting the pain in my ribcage
forgetting my sore ankle and white hair
forgetting I am not as sure-footed
as I once was among dashing strangers

I am mesmerized by a canopy of empty movie reels
corpses of a golden era and confusing relics
to those who someday may unearth them
I'm told this place is earthquake safe
fireproof and bomb safe a mausoleum

station floors are marble and slippery
don't race for a train I silently roar
don't run with a sore ankle or a broken spirit
look at the reels the vintage cars
and Hollywood glitz instead

I turn around slowly and absorb impressions
bold mosaics and message paintings
empty benches and memories
statues with hollow eyes and frozen expressions
movie cameras weeping without film
and some who care and some who don't

over there a young man in a wheel chair
wears a jogging suit and leather half-gloves
and a blank expression like empty movie reels
and faceless sculptures that don't breathe
doors snap open and he disappears
by what miracle whisked away
hooray for Hollywood
the subway and wheelchairs
sore ankles and broken spirits
hooray for back-bent strangers
with full shopping bags pulling them to their knees

I turn quickly and avoid three young men
in the uniform of gangs
their heads shaved their expressions shaved
heavy muscles ripple their arms and calves
and baggy pants hang from crack to ankle
like a heap of laundry thrown around their waists

a swish of cold air
rushes like a live entity down the tracks
then Metrolink's headlight announces its arrival
doors snap open and I tumble back into a car
strangers and I travel toward Mac Arthur Park

back in the tube tired faces
close enough to touch and difficult not to
find their own space

in a rocking train heading for a place
I once went boating with my love

this time I do not disembark
the screech of brakes and brightly painted station
do not tempt me
the train has turned
and I am being propelled
in the bowels of the city going north
back to what is familiar and real

and while the wheels clatter
the world becomes a window of mystery
next to me
in this strangely empty car
I remember the train approaching
like a restless giant
its headlight a blazing sun in the darkness
screech of brakes and warning whistles
muffled chatter
young voices singing
click of heels on marble
sharp blasts of wind
vast murals and bold sculptures
cold paintings
dead movie reels

and into this moment
I know the touch of cool silver poles
breath of strangers
uncertainty
panic of loneliness within a crowd
I will not soon forget

Los Angeles Theater, Downtown

Now and Then I Go to the Movies

stereos blare forth
in a waterfall of sound
splashing over my ears
I sit in dark chambers
popcorn vapors and sticky aisles
my only reminders of childhood

Coming Attractions
dripping with violence
cut into my consciousness
while ghosts from long-ago movies
are only misty and silent creatures
floating in forgotten corners
robbed of their popularity
the giant screen is inescapable
demanding my full attention
I cannot hide from ugliness
or raw emotions magnified
to death-defying dimensions
That's entertainment!

❦

once the theater was a palace
its dimly lit aisles revealing
warm patina of gold filigree
and giant chandeliers
sent dancing lights all around me
then as their crystal elegance slowly dimmed
quivering silence became magical
my heart began to quicken
great crimson drapes slowly parted
unforgettable melodies and vivid colors
became my background of reality
dreams I could become a part of
as the MGM musical began
That was entertainment!

On the Street Where I Lived

time worn jalopies
with dented faces
curbside companions
bumper to bumper
crowd the street

I don't recognize
this narrow street
where my children
roller-skated
played baseball
learned to drive
once alive with adventure
on an expanse of asphalt

tall trees have grown awkwardly
unkempt untrimmed
their roots bulging sidewalks
I remember baby trees
tied to pipe poles
with protective arms of twine
while their branches
bent in spring breezes

my street narrow now
too narrow for cars to pass
once wide and empty
bordered by tract homes
newly painted sparkling in sunlight
unfenced yards endless lawns
free to the wind and mothers' gossip

who came to the street where I lived
who reduced the houses to miniatures
crowded them like toys in a row

I search for 1798 Bushland Street
in the old part of the city
my heart races
I cannot find my home
back and forth I wander
on the street where I lived
my house has disappeared
my home with its wide front lawn
and long driveway to the garage

I search until
fatigue envelopes me
and the scenery is blurred
where is my yellow house
with a red door like lipstick on its face
and smiling Priscilla curtained windows

no it cannot be
this small dirty white plastered place
surrounded by concrete blocks
forming a foot high fence
like a frown around the dying lawn

the curb sign says 1798
my memories jumble
sadness with disbelief
where is there left to search
what became of the home
I knew for twenty-five years
on the street where I lived

Visiting Skirball Museum

echoes
encased in glass shrines
or behind polished woods

Bubbie's babushka turned
smoothly over her forehead
doors and windows bolted in fear

Zayda's head covered
with a moth-eaten felt cap
he was a rabbi in Poland

echoes again in Skirball's halls
what once was
and always will remain

in centuries of tradition

voices I knew
my father's square stained finger
dipped in Passover wine
his prayer chanted in Hebrew

Friday sundown
my mother bent over Sabbath candles
her bushy hair uncovered
her blessing whispered

voices I knew echoing

ornate Chanukah menorahs
in Skirball's simple cases
still speaking of childhood's innocence
frail voices singing
in celebration of faith
most sacred of artifacts
from humble to ornate
a history of my people

and in some forgotten corners
sometimes barely visible
sometimes a small stone in a vast mosaic
an echo of my own family's voice

Frozen in Time

The Cornfield, Antietam

a blanket of snow
covers dried leaves and crimsoned soil
can thirsty earth ever forget
carnage without compromise
in white silence
covering a landscape
long unaccustomed to cannon fire
and lost screams

suddenly a sharp wind howls
where few are there to hear
brother against brother
from the same womb delivered
to this
while bitter cold
guards their tomb today
and no one cheers

Lincoln's Statue, Washington DC

Lincoln's eyes seem to follow me
I climb steps slowly
fearful of falling back
into the star-encrusted night

stone eyes cannot see
still the marble has a soul
cold over an anguished past
a model of undaunted purpose

it is late and lights dim
around the massive sculpture
he looks past my lowered head
toward the reflecting pool

Lincoln's eyes no longer follow me
slowly I descend the slippery steps
fearful of falling
into a starless future

Pause in the Pageantry

Pennsylvania Ave, Washington D.C.

A Prayer

changes in the midst
voices still heard
voices of America
speaking of the beauty and truths
speaking of survival
speaking of growth and conscience

changes in faces and facts
played as a drama
amidst turmoil
against a tapestry of truth
and spirit and integrity
America's strong fabric

in conscience and concern
may those who guide be guided
mountains remaining majestic
waters clean and calm
a sky clear of destruction
hearts cleansed of malice and greed
and our country's unity reflecting its heritage

Beacon on Coast Highway

Point Cabrillo

an image exists
in confusion with the past
as once a wayward sailor
followed a beam of light
flickering through streams of spray
and into the heart of darkness
with a promise

now once more visible
in midnight's moonlight
immobile and protected
from storms and blinding fog
white paint reflecting lunar glow
in indigo stillness

no ships pass by
waters are calm
sky meets sea without controversy
lights within the lighthouse blink
against a curtain of silence
and the wayward sailor
is a long forgotten story

No One Wears Tennis Shoes in Boston

Spring has wrapped her arms
around the Boston Commons
I sit outside on a chipped wooden bench
and watch students clad in wool
hurrying along gusty pathways
in the old city's chilly April
and I am intrigued by what I don't see
for no one wears tennis shoes in Boston

clunky black sandals
stamp over rusty grates
long woolen coats flap
against polished boots
dark skinned loafers
thick-soled and scuffed
meet tweed skirts
and no one strolls about in tennis shoes in Boston

sweatshirt hooded students
whispering academics
bend like saplings in the wind
while nearby twisted branches
softened by new greenery
battle the same icy gusts
trash skitters across sparse lawns
finally trapped against benches and curbs
and statues in the Commons
yet no tennis shoes race from Spring winds in Boston

aging fruit trees
thickly frosted with pink blossoms
release petal showers as they shiver
and tulip patches beneath them
revel silently in their own perfection

while young girls dance nearby in brown oxfords
their faces whipped by scarves and hair
still no tennis shoes pirouette on Boston sidewalks

clumps of students their focus lost
in the wind's sharp gusts
haul laptops into steamy coffee shops
old buildings reeking with neglect
erase the fresh scent of youth
who rush toward the T's

train doors snap open
loading leather shod students
young commuters in careless queues
pushing against strident voices
and bodies stiffened with cold
their arms clutching textbooks
their eyes cast downwards
towards scuffed and worn boots

and in the sun-lit ripples
on path or walk or street
along the leaf-strewn curbs
and windswept brick courtyards
leading to darkly entered hallways
no tennis shoes can be seen in Boston this chilly day

I sit outside on a chipped wooden bench
and watch with awe as people pass by
I look for something oddly missing
afternoon chill numbs me and
I stamp my worn white tennis shoes
against the frost as I wander away
in search of anonymity
and a warm coffee shop
where no one wears tennis shoes today

Rose Avenue
Venice Beach 1935

waves reach far ashore
sometimes
the porch shudders in salty wind
sometimes
clouds scatter on the horizon line
sometimes
the rocker sits waiting
always

When I was little, maybe seven or eight, we spent our summers in a smelly dark apartment on Rose Avenue in Venice Beach and called it a *vacation.* Our home for July and August was half of a duplex, whose one redeeming feature, aside from being a block from the beach, was its wide front porch.

Early afternoons I used to change into a scratchy woolen bathing suit and follow my mother and brother Lionel down across the ocean front walk, skipping over the hot sand to the wonderful relief of the Pacific Ocean's fingers of foam.

I remember the sharp sting of the water as I backed into the surf. I remember running away and screaming as the ripples pulled into a giant wall of green and I barely escaped the next lashing wave.

The joy of it, the utter abandonment, the hot, sticky, salty sweetness of it left me singing and dancing in circles.

Showering and spreading Noxema over my sun-burned back, I finally snuggled into soft flannel pajamas. I recall listening to Jack Benny and eating cream cheese and jelly sandwiches, sipping hot cocoa, eventually drifting off to the muffled sounds of the sea and the squeak of our rocking chair in the early evening breeze.

waves reach far ashore
sometimes
the porch shudders in salty wind
sometimes
clouds scatter on the horizon line
sometimes
the rocker sits waiting
always

❧

My Pen is a Paintbrush

words evolve from reality to fantasy

tinsel the ordinary

balance lights and darks

My Pen is a Paintbrush

CONTENTS

Painter's Dream 219
Transparent 220
My Pen is a Paintbrush 221
Yosemite, Once Home
    of the Miwok 222
Forest Graveyard 224
Exploring the Redwoods. 225
Retreat. 226
Noble Stance 227
View from My Kitchen Window. . 228
Window "Pain" 229
Windy Day in Chatsworth 230
Bea's Wildflowers 232
Desert Sketches 234
Inspiration 235
Survival 236
Crescendo. 237
Moods in Gray 238
Temporary Waters 239
Colorado Cloud Paintings 240
Twilight Meeting 242
Tenacity 243
Autumn Performance 244
October 245
Later. 246
Waiting for Dawn 247

Canyon Lights. 248
Reunion 249
Harmony 250
Whispering Gardens 251
Japanese Gardens in the Rain. . . 252
Tranquility 253
Mystery 254
Eagle's Flight 255
Laguna's Shore 256
Where Sea Meets Land 257
Beach Morning. 258
Cliff View 259
Sky Tears 260
Hidden Canyon Lake 261
Idaho December 262
Maryland's Winter 263
Within a Frame. 264
Mountain Stream in Winter 265
Above Me 266
First Rainfall. 267
Cloud Shadows 268
Spring 269
Horizontal Rain 270
April Morning. 271
Visions of Color and Grace 272
A Lone Fish. 274

Painter's Dream

would your brush meet mine
swirl around in paint
threads of color crossing
and choreograph
dances with subtle patterns

if the canvas were near
might we not greet it
cloud the stark reality
while jewels of color blossom

is that a landscape you have chosen
still shimmering uncertain in sunlight
I prefer bold strokes biting colors
will they spoil the tenderness

I dream of dark and light and sunsets
canvas constantly changing
our colors are mixed
brushes poised
can you stop the splattering
and confine them

Transparent

through the narrow lens of my vision
through a transparent window of perception
do I know the world around me
am I able to perceive reality with crisp clarity
no matter the disguise
no matter my limited sight

I am grateful for brilliant sunsets
rolling green hills
seas of jade and blue and silver
still what have I missed
in a moment unrecognized

what exists beyond the sun's glow
crawls among the hill's grasses
struggles beneath the sea's serene surface
what moves and whispers with life
and remains unseen and unheard

My Pen is a Paintbrush

words
capture colors
frame fading rainbows
interpret subtle shadings
evolve from reality to fantasy
tame unbridled sunlight
tinsel the ordinary
balance lights and darks
sketch gestalt galaxies
become whimsical washes
brush gold into sunsets
highlight Fall's finery
and blend
into a word painting

Yosemite, Once Home of the Miwok

quaking aspen
singing leaves
quiver in new-born breezes
silver birch
fettered to the landscape
bend over in whistling wind tunnels
ribbons of dark green trees
scatter along the valley's gray carpet

antlers of snow
perch on mountain tops
remnants of winter storms
resisting melt down
slate cathedral walls below
divide sunlight into brilliant beams
while plants struggle in hidden crevices
and cling to life
existing on sparse lichen
and morning dew

granite sculptures hardening
in earth's bowels
erupted like giants
reaching for the sun
centuries in their struggle to emerge
then remain gouged into shapes
by blades of ice

far within the near landscape
of Yosemite finery
water plunges restlessly
over granite obstacles
preaching the gospel
of its magnanimous spirit

waterfalls insisting on power
and strength as persuasion
capture run-off from mountain giants

and spill with joy
over boulders and fallen trees
over shiny submerged rocks
finally bubbling across sand and pebbles
into quiet lakes

in the distance hidden waterfalls
are covered with
smoky garlands of mist
mysterious in their shifting moods
spirits surrounding all
Miwok legends cling to ancient trees
and rock formations
and rushing waters
whisper in tongues long forgotten
and drift into the present
like snow flurries in spring

while far above
within walls of a granite cathedral
only silent prayers exist
no words uttered by indestructible voices
a face in magnificent profile
there among the clouds
above the falcon's nest
above intervention by sterile spirits

Forest Graveyard

Mammoth, California

still proud in death's garb
standing in sparse rows
clinging to identity once verdant
once clothed in emeralds
and winter's diamonds

pale beyond recognition
some still bent in agony
others lying twisted on the ground
a few barren forms upright
held there by roots tangled
in unforgiving soil

dead trees not charred by fire
not cut by commercial blades
lonely faded sentinels
destroyed by unknown poisons
emanating from a witch's brew
beneath the earth's crust
strangling life
from each one growing there

memory of tall mountain trees
once facing dawn with courage

Exploring the Redwoods

leaves crunch thickly
beneath my feet
and muffle my footsteps
with their depth
while I enter a forest
of ancient living trees

girth of trunk
roughness of bark
speak with voices of assurance
where past and present meet
in thunder and in silence
giants challenging
a tranquil landscape

redwoods stand solidly
through corridors of history
and greet me now as I recall
those early explorers
who found strength in forests
constant in a changing world

Retreat

down this path
step by step
slippery rocks
dry leaves crushed
tangled roots snaking across
the sandy creek bed

I return
to the green and thick forest floor
where soil comforts and enriches
sun and rain are friends

down this path
step by step
following leaves that sing
and a hidden stream
whispering its secrets

Noble Stance

you are here
not a speaking entity
your voice still discernible
in a forest of brothers

you are rooted
still moving
arms reaching
toward the sky
leaves turning
to welcome the sun

I can feel your presence
roughness of your bark
nobility of your stance
protection of your shade
strength of your tenacity

View from My Kitchen Window

(After Northridge Earthquake 1994)

red tile roofs
form a pattern
touching an undefined cloud filled sky
birds perch on horizontal wires
another pattern broken
by recently trimmed trees

bricks march evenly
across high cement walls
their patterns reflected
in shadows below

empty flower pots hang
in debris strewn patios
and birds chirp looking for nests
in eaves once again

a wisteria vine clinging to life
shares a bloom a touch of color
while far below
the trash stained blacktop
bears witness to construction
still in progress

Window "Pain"

my picture window is streaked
with rivulets of rain and grime
as I gaze out at my patio

plants are waving echoes
no longer dusted with summer's sand
rose bushes struggle in the torrents
their scattered petals pasted to pavement
a broken chair a shattered table
no elegance remains in streams of water
my patio is strewn with debris
crayons twirling in puddles
soggy newspapers with blurred headlines
an ice-cream wrapper and a gold star

cascades of water
finally swallow mud
and sweep shattered glass
broken tiles and pieces of wood
symbolic of wind's fury
toward the gate
and glittering shards
become blinding bits of mirror
when sunlight breaks through

Windy Day in Chatsworth

the wind calls to me
pushes through falling leaves
and sends pewter chimes
into dissonant clinking
against my patio wall

I open my door
gingerly at first
then boldly to accept
the cool slap of frosted air
crashing down from canyon halls

the sky is swept clear
of rain cloud debris
only a few feathers remain
twirling around aimlessly
scattering into oblivion

ancient trees on Dupont street
bend painfully in sharp gusts
shuddering with their effort
their top-heavy branches struggle
against the wind's unforgiving force

birds escape, flying in a V
heading south
their songs no longer heard
amidst swishing and wailing
when suddenly stillness covers
plants and trees and chimes

in that moment
the giant holds his breath
then just as suddenly
all is set in motion again
as I close my door against the onslaught

Bea's Wildflowers

2000

traffic rumbles
down Burbank Boulevard
with a screech and a roar
while twittering birds
continue their melodic mayhem
and hover over
a wildflower garden
circling Bea's driveway

flowers grown from seeds
blown to the damp soil
in confusion
rooting and thriving
join in a lacy network
of cornflowers and poppies
lupines and daisies
and dance through dry leaves
fallen from the nearby oak tree

blooms bravely smiling
face the dusty asphalt driveway
and taunt traffic
breezes move flowers
into a living picture
shyly welcoming me
at my old friend's door

2010

where are they now
those colorful bouquets
reduced to words
reduced to dust
seedlings blown away
seeking life
away from a house
abandoned in foreclosure

Desert Sketches

silent arms
cut through
thin desert air
energy consumed
somewhere else

mountain outlines
penciled into dusk
gray purple then brown
shadings crumble
to the desert floor
and dust bushes with haze
in the shadows

night animals roam
claiming redemption
in the harsh reality
of desert rock and sand
seek shelter
relieve thirst
adapting in chameleon colors

Inspiration

Chatsworth Hills are nude
shadows sculpt dry slopes
and outline rugged borders
against a windswept sky

a pulse remains in stillness
awakens in movement
perceptible only after centuries
boulders begin to loosen

Chatsworth Hills are nude
painted in dusk's colors
inviting an artist's brush
or a poet's pen

Survival

one sentinel
taller than the rest
aged and growing barren
his crown broken
by some primal wind
or merely the ravages of time

one elder statesman
outlined against blue and purple
his shadow mingling
with the others
and extending beyond them
remains rooted to the earth

below ferns flourish
with strength in rich soil
while young trees
providing scarce shade
refuse to be bowed
by spring winds
and reach upward
toward a bright sky

Crescendo

tremulous rustle at first
motionless branches begin to stir
dry leaves creep along pathways

wind whips flags
shredding their pride
tears through tree tops
shatters frozen twigs

rush of cold air
orchestration of movement
sigh of retreat
silence

Moods in Gray

what can I say
this day of overcast and gray
mist clinging to branches and covering my eyelids

worn wooden clapboards
of my childhood
dirty snow
tossed cavalierly
on my porch
and washed into rain puddles
later prayers
turning gray drops into pearls

clouds curtaining the sun
and silvered nonetheless
a soft rumble
part of the wind
and driven rain
heard somewhere behind
an ominous wall of gray

what can I say
this day of overcast and gray
mist clinging to branches and covering my eyelids

Temporary Waters

a pond the color of mud
yellow and brown and murky
holding thunder shower drain-off
in a broken cup of swirls

air heavy with moisture
releasing redolent scents of rain-washed flowers
sprinkles on coffee-cream waters
and a mother duck's progeny

tails up diving for worms
far away from a park's cool lake
shy swimmers shaded by a few green branches
and visited by a cardinal's cry

a muddied pond short lived
in Maryland's humid landscape
yet alive with purpose as some
seek food and shelter
in its temporary waters

Colorado Cloud Paintings

cloud shadows
cool mountain slopes
in August's warm dawn

clouds piled like snow
gently cover young aspens
on the Rockies' rim

rain air redolent
with damp earth smells
dark veils of moisture
linger at dusk

nimbus clouds float
like great gray parachutes
down over the springs

cumulus clouds billow
into a zoo of shapes
constantly transforming
the sky's landscape

lonely wisps of clouds
drift like feathers
suddenly abandoned within
a vast canopy above us

☙

sunlight polishes the blue
into gleaming perfection
trims clouds with silver
or burns
through gray masses
like smoke radiating
into an endless dome
smudging its perfection

જી

blue paint white paint gray paint
great blobs
trails of feather wisps
brush strokes in arcs
skyscapes

Twilight Meeting

branches
tall network of dark wires
pressed into a fading sky
birds
flutter in v's
like a waving hand
change direction
then scatter onto twigs
and become black lace
bordering the sunset

Tenacity

parched land
denuded of greenery
dead and charred
leaves and branches

ancient winds
sweep yellow plains
and disturb ashes
silence frames burned bushes
screaming at lifeless twigs

sky meets land
in lonely blending
relentless heat sparks
yet another blaze

where once water nourished them
new roots do not survive
and there amidst blackened corpses
Kookaburra still squawks in protest

El Nino causes heavy rains
in California and a drought in Australia

Autumn Performance

a spotlight shimmers
down from mountain peaks
creeps toward clustered pines
highlights their elegance
all framed by Fall's curtain
trembling yellow orange crimson
above an ancient fallen tree
resting peacefully
on a lake's rock strewn shore

water caresses a log
laps at the mud-painted grass
while a bird
shy actress in the spotlight
perches on the dry side
of a fallen tree

October

solitude
motionless
and alive
with barely perceptible pulse
wind chimes
in the distance

dried leaves drift away
from lonely branches
a flutter of sound
muted in frosted dawns

loneliness
without regret
within a gray frame
crystal reflections

memories
awakened in Fall
energy
diffused from dreams

October evening
canopy of stars
cool velvet night
embroidered with music
wind chimes
in the distance

Later

winter was a time
I used to feel
a rough warmth
in sweaters
icy chill of new snow

after something closed the door
on Fall
quietly with the softest click
and a gentle swirl
of dry and fresh leaves
around my ankles

Waiting for Dawn

lights and darks
reflect leaves
like sun-lit coins

black fades
into pewter
into a monochromatic mystery

leaves quiver
whispering
voices within foliage
shadows without form

tree twigs
dressed in flimsy black lace
brush a silver sky

branches
snake like graceful dancers
behind a curtain of leaves
in a moonlit spotlight

a hidden forest
ebony trunks
enjoy solitude
waiting for dawn

Canyon Lights

light from the setting sun
floats like a golden scarf
over striated ridges
burns through shadows
brightens crimson streaks
along canyon walls

diffused light hovers
like a sensuous whisper
making intimate contact
with rows of cliffs

suddenly touches of white
a cool reminder of evening mist
brush over rocks
and struggling brush

Reunion

the gnarled tree
bent toward the earth
like an old man
in hungry despair
suddenly
a swift young bird
perched upon his tired shoulder
preened her brilliant feathers
then whirred away
leaving an echo
of youth to fall
upon his aging limbs
like warm spring rain

Harmony

reflection of form
of pattern and serenity
each branch
each stone
each blossom
each pool
in harmony
and part of
composite beauty

senses soothed
and delighted
simplicity in sound
and structure
old and new
painted into
a landscape
by an architect
blending into
his own creation

We might have viewed a painting that had been magically transformed into a living thing, or a sculpture bent in the wind and subtly turned toward the sun. For this was not the profusion of nature, but a carefully disciplined creation from its elements.

Whispering Gardens

stillness disturbed
by gently swirling waters
far off cry of crows and
whir of hummingbirds' wings
answering rustle of leaves
beckoning egrets to glide
across the gray canopy of sky
and perch upon the highest branches

golden Koi rearrange the waters
with faint and fading ripples
their color and shape
reflected in the pool's mirror

rocks and stones
bridges and lanterns
stand rooted to the earth
as though experiencing life
quivering around them
music emerges from silence
patterns of leaf and branch
bamboo and wood and clouds
all reflect in waters below
and move into whispering life

Japanese Gardens in the Rain

egrets pose
upon green thrones
at the fragile tops
of Spring's leafy branches
mirrored pools below
reflect stark whiteness
and feathery outline
of spreading wings

mist collects
into fine droplets
and later
rhythmic needles
prick still waters
barely disturbing
their tranquility

forms reposed
in ancient history
rest now
in breathing silence
mutely describing
what once was
in nature's music
and fragile blossoms

while stone lanterns
and bridges remain
etched as a picture
against a gray sky

Tranquility

no one disturbs
my thoughts here
alone I can close my eyes and visualize
each rock and leaf
reflected in a pool of silence

no tears blur
a simple landscape
or thundering heartbeat
intrude upon the calm
of sculpted greenery
silhouetted against
a cloud-free sky

singing birds are hidden
I hear them briefly
and they blend
into the rustle of leaves
within reeds and young plants
meeting the pool's edge

and the turmoil within me
subsides

I sit quietly on a stone bench
near the pool's edge
foreign to the landscape
still part of it

Mystery

where is this place
of restless reflections
and fiery skies
melting into a mirrored lake

who carved sculptures
bold and sunlit
anchored in murky depths
and silhouetted
against a molten sky

who sets eddies in motion
so subtle
a shadow erases them
and only traces of sunlight
reveal intricate patterns

their mystery solved
as night approaches
reality emerges slowly
with brown and gray rocks
in a mountain pool at dusk

Eagle's Flight

stillness mirrored
in stark images
painting an icy pool

dark mountains fade
into snow brushed summits
there veiled in uncertain clouds

glistening ice peaks
emerge from shadowed pools
and reach upward
with naked arms
toward a lone eagle
a giant bird
focused in flight
supported by subtle currents
in the silver landscape

Laguna's Shore

shoreline's fringe
wide lacy arcs
sand islands
smoothed into wet mirrors

pewter sky
overlaid with silver stripes
miles of surf
so tender
gulls skid along easily
before ascending

surfers like black sea birds
balance on wave crests
pose in silhouette
before they tumble
rolling like lost children
in ocean swirls

sand bars
long searching arms
reach into the sea
calmly with no motion
in their tenacity

the sea
wrinkled landscape
silver satin spread over miles
floats in waning light
and covers a sleeping giant

Where Sea Meets Land

sea meets land
washes over shell strewn shores
ripple upon ripple
wave pushing wave
white tipped
suddenly crashing
then spent
receding
foam fingers left in damp sand

tide pools remain
swirls of debris and crabs
children with tin buckets
collect shells
dig for crabs
build sand castles
the sea
a far off roar

Beach Morning

mist rises from the sea
waves crash and recede
like brass cymbals at dawn

sands ease into relaxed ripples
and reach the water
in widening arcs
disappearing in froth

sandpipers skitter over
sand mirrors and move in circles
across the beach
patches of seaweed glimmer
like jewels on the shore

smear of clouds across the sky
tames the sun's insistent brilliance
pelicans skim and dive
with relaxed arrogance

sunlight suddenly throws
a net of sparkles across the sea
dolphins play Hide and Seek
as they swim up the coast
seagulls descend in graceful arcs
and alight on warming sands

waves crash and recede
like brass cymbals
greeting the day

footprints on wet sand
mark my way to the sea
where I seek to reclaim
moments of childhood

Cliff View

rocks jut out
like lingering giants
bathing in swirling waters
tasting foam

prisoners still yearning
for indigo and silver waters
deeper mysteries

sometimes submerged
beneath the sea's roiling surface
later left by retreating tides
to dry into bronze and gold statues
in the sunlight

Sky Tears

raindrops are tears
barely trickling along sidewalks
in sad rivulets through dust
joining each other
in small puddles

raindrops are tears
torrential driven showers
washing away dry leaves
and old memories
in staccato rhythm on sidewalks

raindrops are tears
only misty reminders
leaving enough transparent space
to reflect rainbows
in a newly washed sky

Hidden Canyon Lake

I stand in cool waters
their gentle movement
creating eddies around my ankles
purple silence around me
interrupted by shy splashing
twilight painted ripples
against the pebbled shore

I stand in cool waters
and look up at a cathedral rising
from my shadowed present
slate and dark rocks

above me
striated purples grays pinks
leading to the golden rim

suddenly my mood rises
without wings or reason
like a young bird
in soaring flight
upward

Idaho December

leaden sky
underlined by pale brushstrokes
geometric interruptions
roof tops strung
with green red and gold
colored halos
in a lonely
Christmas dusk

fingers of snow
creep across
wrinkled black hills
nude in Winter's chill
melting mounds
surround sparkling neon signs
sand scratched roads
and patches of black ice

wind stretches gray clouds
into thin banners
across a fading sky
lifeless flatlands rest
damp uncaring
piles of dead grass and twigs
gingerly crossed by skittering quail
in wingless flight

Maryland's Winter

Winter sky's disarray of clouds
send snow flurries scurrying
in their own direction
ice crystals glaze naked limbs
while a dusting of white
equalizes asphalt roads
and worn porch clapboards

I do not know cold intimately
only briefly in Maryland's landscape
the icy layer
between my sleeves and bare skin
like an insistent stranger
to my senses
while silence drifts
with flakes of snow
and fallen leaves
along deserted streets

Within a Frame

serenity blooms in snow
whispers of silence
float in crystal air
too subtle to be noticed
afraid in a bold gray sky
only faintly heard
above the cabin's crackle
burning logs

clouds settle noiselessly
on the mountain's rim
and slowly come to rest
with a sigh

trees stand guard
wearing shining white armor
and face the wind's fury

inside rustic cabins
colors deepen
dance in firelight
voices rise and fall
and life is unaware
of the frame
within which it is painted

Mountain Stream in Winter

snow capped boulders
sleeping giants
washed by icy whispering eddies
their hard reality softened
where foamy splashes
lift away crusts of white

tall sentinels
quiver on the shore
silver tipped branches reach
toward a leaden sky
waters below continue to swirl
with hushed voices
in the wintry silence

Above Me

clouds are shifting once more
their borders rearranged
like bolts of white silk
rippling through the sky
frayed edges trimmed
with silver

First Rainfall

drizzle descends slowly
like a curtain of jewels
drapes over dusty bushes
droplets cling
to each leaf
a sudden breeze
shakes them loose
sparkles into the mist

Cloud Shadows

I search the sky's expanse
and realize every moment changing
casts shadows on nearby hills
shadows
giant veils of mystery drift off
revealing a sun
splintering the skyline

clouds drape my landscape
at their whim
like a mist of tears
then part curtains
for the sunlight
illuminating the land with promises
emerging from darkness

like dreams clouds skip through my vision
never remaining in one form
one idea to grasp
subtle sometimes unreadable
an unpredictable future

clouds float above earth's reality
rest on lofty mountain peaks
beyond my reach
below a jet's roar

their illusive forms always changing
cumulous nimbus cirrus
constantly re-arranged
calming the sun's fury
satisfying the earth's thirst
shadowing the landscape

Spring

alabaster faces
hidden in a crystalline spring
winter's icicles
tangled in the underbrush

frozen drops
join a string of jewels
decorating branches
like spring blossoms

faces somewhere
amidst new-grown greenery
illuminated
by a glowing sun
melt into smiles

Horizontal Rain

thunder resounds in soft moist air
bird sounds lost in the ominous roar
while angry clouds invade blue expanses
and erase remaining wisps of white

suddenly a jagged edge of light
illuminates pools of darkness
covering a once tranquil landscape

thunder speaks without restraint
damp air becomes its own voice
combines with screaming wind
and lightning reveals
horizontal rain

April Morning

one morning in April
the sky exploded
into torrents of rain sparkles
birds wove in between streams
the dark arches of their wings
reflected in roadside puddles

one morning in April
a crimson rosebud slowly unfurled
turning toward the sun
stem and leaves bent silently
toward light and life

one morning in April
wind clattered into my life
setting leaves and bells and bits of wood
into a reality of sounds
often silent in the confusion
and first conscious moments of my dawn

one morning in April
the sky was cloudless and faded blue
birds gathered on my window sill
busy with their own gossip
oblivious to the notes of my song
lost within their own harmonies

Visions of Color and Grace

Discovery

I saw a white butterfly today
drifting like a scrap of paper
wings closed barely lifted
by a whisper of breeze

smaller than the rose petal
upon which it had paused
in brief respite
from restless fluttering

too small to meet my gaze
a wisp a smile a poem
disappearing into Spring's arms
like a prayer of renewal

A Magic Moment

the butterfly's wings closed
as it perched lightly
a whisper on my arm

its fragile form
trembled with life
a rare glimpse
of beauty once common,
a moment of magic
before it floated away barely visible
in the bright sunlight
and shadowed pattern of leaves

Peacock's Accolade

from silence and submission
flared into color
quivering with life
in feathered drama
eyes staring
with relentless bravado
a bold fan of iridescence
waiting and challenging

A Lone Fish

shafts of sunlight
penetrate mysterious shadows
in deep ocean waters
and radiate into a halo
around a lone fish exploring coral

surprising clarity remains
undisturbed
by murky floating sands
and showers of bubbles
rising to the surface

blues fanning out intensify
and slowly deepen
from powder to azure
indigo to midnight

a solitary fish swims through colors
exploring lacy coral branches
unaware of isolation
in the midst of his discoveries

CHAPTER VII

Any Way You Look at It

for I am old you see
and full of nonsense
any way you look at it

Any Way You Look At It

CONTENTS

Total Recall. 279

Identity 280

Any Way You Look at It 281

Search 282

Relationships 283

Doors 284

Deception. 285

Identification 286

Offerings 287

Flirt 288

Crimson 289

Eyebrows 290

Makeup 291

Masks. 292

Rag Bag 293

Thirteen. 294

A Young Follower of Rock Groups 295

After-Party. 296

Opportunity 297

Death of a Child 298

A Mother's Loss of Faith 299

The Other Side of the Coin 300

Dream 301

Explanation 302

Betrayal 303

Candle 304

Coffee Cup 305

Direction 306

Message. 307

Desolation 308

Politicians 309

Protest 310

Floodlights. 311

Inertia 312

Decisions 313

Military Graveyard 314

Return in Winter. 315

Clock 316

Clowns 317

Changing Tides 318

And Disappear 319

Who Rides My Yellow Pony 320

Relatively. 321

Interruption 322

Goal 323

Age. 324

I've Lost It for the Moment. 325

Time Changes. 326

Silence 327

The Far Side 328

Total Recall

paper thin memories
crumble before me
too delicate to retain their texture
just a glimpse on tissue
before the text turns to dust

if once viewed
only for a second
if once articulated
only in a whisper
then a picture must remain
however dim
or frayed at the edges
images speaking without words

my body and intellect experienced
boldly and painfully and joyfully
that time was real
pain vivid
joy overflowing
music embracing me

where is the path
I once so cavalierly followed
where did it lead
I still remember wild flowers
winking on the side of the road
and my pen is ready

Identity

roots in unyielding clay
trapped in its density
and moistened
only enough to survive

below withered
leaves and stems
under surface tensions
still there in a tangled pattern

unreachable barriers
sticks broken
pointed in opposing directions
no new passage or rivulet
to reach the pale strands

Any Way You Look at It

fling out those worried phrases
a rainstorm of protest
little creatures know better
when they crawl through dust
I haven't begun to look for you
all I have is a photograph
and some nonsensical phrases
don't warn me
don't even jump over all those
sticks and stones
the rainbow's promise will tempt you
but not me
certainly not me
for I'm old you see
and full of nonsense
any way
you look at it

❧

Search

for those of you who find
the lonely retreat I have fashioned
from clay of past hidden rewards
your jewels are pressed
into hardening reality
I cannot pluck them out
so strongly are they bonded
to forgotten tales

begin your immobile journey
in paralyzing tranquility
while gulls gash the wayward sky
and calligraphy of noises announces
departure of friend and enemy
clarify who remains
and close the volume

Relationships

how strange are the ties that bind
sister to brother
friend to friend
and discover
the threads are but spider webs
so easily brushed away
by anger or neglect
or the passage of time

some woven into steel from silken threads
some invincible except in certain light
some catching fire in troubled sunset
then disappearing from its waning warmth

I cannot unravel the threads
or understand their intricate patterns
just as a spider I weave them
just as a fly I am entangled

Doors

closed doors
broken locks
passed by
without curiosity

some recently slammed
welcome signs lying
cracked and splintered
as I trip over the debris

doors shaking ominously
in their fragile frames
about to come loose
and collapse in their own dust

closed doors
just off the road shutting quickly
when I changed my mind
about to turn back

open doors opened by my hand
or someone else's
designed to entice and invite
warm to the touch

open doors
revealing rooms
too blazing in color
to be tolerated

doors ajar
hidden by dark shadows
demanding to be
explored again

Deception

this you said you knew
for sure and I believed you

why not when it was so easy
like dunking for apples

then surprise
at the icy water
and choking impossibility
of success

Identification

a leaf skeleton covers my finger print
their patterns both uniquely designed
each history etched in ovals and arcs
delicacy belying strength
loss of youth and life redefined
my fingers crush the leaf
and what was once recognized
by its green skin and place in the sun
now so fragile it cannot survive
returns to dust
weightless and flicked away

Offerings

imperfect packages
ill-gotten illusions
tied in ribbons
of uncertainty

wrinkled remembrances
smeared ink
over patterned wrappings
old bargains
and tattered price tags

Flirt

Hi there! he said
I turned just enough
for a sideways glance

slowly his profile knifed its way
into my conscious moment
remembering today's toxic tensions
I turned away myself
toward better fortunes

Crimson

I left my polish at Max's house
how could I do such a thing
when the red lacquer goes where I go

after all chipped nails
will never do
and the red-tipped perfection
of manicured fingers
is the quintessential expression
of confidence and courage
if I am to meet my world
half-way

Eyebrows

arched as birds' wings
mysterious and mystifying
comment and commentary

pencil gliding over
guiding each line
guiding expressions
and expressing
grief and surprise

eyes questioning
eyebrows frame questions
arched with concern
and drawn by a whimsical hand

my hand guiding paint or pencil
over nature's original intent
my eyebrows hide
behind a glass frame
and smudge it
with a bit of color

Makeup

is the face a canvas
empty flesh unlined unwritten
something missing
in the smooth expanse
neatly measured
over bone and sinew

eyes open slowly
tentatively
seeing nothing
until a paintbrush
dots a widening pupil

is the face a canvas
seeking pink cheeks
slash of red lipstick
emerald shadowed eyelids
ready to respond
contours carefully painted
visible palette
personality defined

Masks

it is not easy for me to smile
not that I don't find joy and humor
still my particular mask
has lips only slightly parted
and a twinkling eye almost hidden

it is not easy for me to cry
for tears draw my eyelids closed
and swim within their dark orb
my mask is serene
withdrawn revealing nothing

it is not easy for me to be angry
with a mask stiff and confining
stretched across a fiery soul
bands of steel pushing
firmly against the embers

Rag Bag

silver sequins
on my torn sweater

torn cardigan beginning to unravel
can I remember the words
if not the text
emotions that rip apart quietly
like a bird's muffled cry in the night

I might capture that bird
comprehend its song
feel pulse within its body
know it is a living thing
to be set free before restraints
injure it

what are memories made of
a bird's heartbeat
an old sweater
silver viewed as tarnished

unraveling knit
first only a pulled thread
one of many
threads holding silver sequins
one by one falling
at my feet below my vision
because I do not wish to look there

shiny silver sequins
in a glittering pile
free of yarn scraps
just beyond where I choose
to remember

Thirteen

with hopscotch innocence engaged
in carefree laughter
seeking anonymity
behind a tree trunk
or under a porch slat
Oli, oli, oxen free free free...
gliding on the wind's surface
You won't catch me.
You can't catch me.

in Spring's flower-strewn redolence
a garland wound through her hair
she approaches a precipice
adolescence entered
mirrors clouded with smoke
and cracked
rap music shattering their clarity
until jagged edges
strip the last vestige of innocence
and songs of childhood
are only an echo

❦

A Young Follower of Rock Groups

weave songs into a gypsy's shawl
and colored threads tell a story
of pauper's jokes
while trashy icons
appear like blue lipped angels
never comprehending their misfortune
and chanting with evangelistic fervor

all her beads and bracelets
blaze with irony on pale arms
in the waning sunlight
and drum-driven wishes
gather strength in a starless night
needy trespassers cling to frayed edges
as if their rasping voices
could harmonize with rapture
between the silken threads

After-Party

I have so many friends
on this star-strewn path
leaping like dandelions in the wind
all around my wavering purpose

they are invincible
and kinder than failure would be
to me alone this time
this moment

we whirl around impossible turns
lost in confusion
lost here
never assuming a universal truth
garments torn
garments of illusions
stitched together once more

Opportunity

my eyes shaded from the sun
I search between cloud formations
blueness there is illuminated
by silver

beyond mystery surrounds
an illusive place
where gray mists intrude upon
and sometimes hide
fleeting light I know is there

a promise
tremulous in its message
insisting on visibility
constantly re-appearing

Death of a Child

it's time to cry
you said that day
when one had left
and one had died

sun is ice
you said that day
and ripped it from
the raging sky

moon's glow too bright
you said that night
and tore the light
in anguished shreds

stars are gone
you said that dawn
when one had left
and one had died

A Mother's Loss of Faith

alone has rained a storm
and blinded me

now the arc has opened
a faint rustle of bells
silver bells above red velvet
destitute opulence
reach out and touch
touch and kiss
I can't   I can't   I can't
I cannot do this

my child brushed the crimson
with his innocence
rain has frozen on his face

I am lost in sorrow
and sorrowful for my loss

The Other Side of the Coin

there on the asphalt
hidden amongst debris
like a broken promise
stepped on with disregard
for it's only a penny

face hidden beneath dirt and leaves
tarnished with wear
scarred with misuse
once a shiny replica of Lincoln
now turned toward the gritty walkway

perhaps a child will stumble upon it
or an old man's cane pry it loose
perhaps the rain will dislodge it
and float it away
from its lonely retreat
and into the sunlight

Dream

dream is reality
waking up the dream
flickers of fantasy
demonic uncertainty
frayed memories
blurred like fading watercolors

I am falling gently
wondrously
stop   stop
this room is cold
a shivering loft
peopled by princes without faces
cardboard figures

where
I can't remember
I can't remember

Explanation

wild purgatory
grass spiders
inch their way to
a resolution of webs

find the slovenly slave owners
reminisce and seize
the explanation
like a prayer of angels
hovering in metric certainty
unaware

Betrayal

my friend is here by touch
an only star when the moon
has disappeared
I collect misgivings
and watch them
silver pressed
through pinholes
blended
then asleep
in the questioning
dawn of trust

Candle

red gold flame
feel its presence
experience its warmth
hypnotized
back away
just enough

flickering light can distort
warmth can be deceiving
and candle wax can melt
into a misshapen mass

Coffee Cup

how many times a cup of coffee

consolation
inspiration
conversation

and then coldness
aloneness
taste of bitterness
brewed darkness

nothing left to share

Direction

up is up
and down is up
yesterday jumps like a puppet
and puppets are stiff
but strings aren't
funny
isn't it

Message

frown of clouds
obscures the moon
thunder resounds
with an organ's fury
dark deep ominous tones
uncompromising
lightening strikes
illuminating my thoughts
warning me
of complacency's folly

Desolation

a cheek of alabaster
crying to the ferocious
decanters
full of emeralds
rattling in confines
too stiff in glaring sunlight

sea water
gulping at the crisis
each needle
lying wasted
camouflaged
in sand crystals
dry as dust
and near ocean sounds

Politicians

chaotic brotherhood
of power and pretense
nominating symbols
in the conflicted confusion

of colors

shake my hand
look me squarely in the eye
fly me into space
with conflicted confusion

of colors

lead me oh mentors
with songs and flags
and words melting at the edges
with conflicted confusion

of colors

Protest

friendly figures forage
through glass grasses
each blade
a perilous point of contention

I rummage through the painter's rags
torn and stained
still camouflaged
and shredded by
a vast community of doubt
I still remember
the scaffolds were high
above the littered brilliant sparkling shards

one figure fell
too far for us to recognize his journey
or even locate what he left behind
for the friendly foragers to find

Floodlights

watch out
their brilliance
can blind you
it's worse when
there are more than one
and any way
you turn your face
no side is shadowed

beams can move
quickly
faster than you can
dodge them now
soon you won't care
about the light

Inertia

he hasn't questioned
lately at least
and the webs grow
thick and sticky

watch there
between the smallest
threaded squares
hardly any movement
at all

Decisions

desperate pathways
incongruous decisions
like solitude of terror
in an atmosphere of shooting stars
forgive my garland of withered roses
corpses of the future
dried out along unexplored
trails
all in sepia
frail hands not quite reaching
across the chasm of forgetfulness
questioning in silent voices

Military Graveyard

drumbeat heartbeat echoes
echoes calling echoes
train whistles taunt the solitude
gunsmiths pound metal to metal
crying

once in the calmness of midnight
gather the wilted flowers
gather the cannon volleys
gather the crosses and stars
stained and warped wood

one dreary footprint
encased in mud
drumbeat heartbeat echoes

Return in Winter

prisoners behind
bars of grief in prism houses
birds
dots on winter dead branches
abandoned nests barely supported
by icy twigs about to snap

frozen smiles on frozen faces
torn black ribbons cling
to oak tree trunks
extinguished candles sigh
wisps of smoke escape

Clock

clock ticking
tempting time
teasing
beckoning
continuous
reckoning

Clowns

the clowns are here
painted faces
false smiles
cartwheels of candor
inappropriate tears
armfuls of daisies
wilted and wondering
clay-apple misgivings
juggled with uncertainty
smashed in laughter

Changing Tides

seamless sighs
blowing out
like puffs of sorrow

moving across
granules of ashen sand
crushed into dust
withered beach rogues
cross the flooded symmetry

one small crab traverses
scarring the face of wet sand
soon trapped
in gloomy frothing uncertainty
deeply awakened
by possessive tides

And Disappear

children scamper
along bleached sand beaches
chanting
and exploring
abandoned castles
frightened crabs
polished bits of glass

and busy themselves
with popping seaweed blossoms

while their bare footprints
fill with sea water
and disappear

Who Rides My Yellow Pony

who rides my yellow pony

I have been away
long ago days and nights
and just returned
I hear galloping
dust is floating
still my pony is nowhere
to be seen

who rides my yellow pony
yellow is yellow
jonquil yellow
lemon yellow
sun on sand yellow

my pony is special yellow
and he is gone

Relatively

dawn breaks
an inevitable day
emerging through night sounds
a continuous journey
unsheltered by any oasis
time continues
each day in slow motion
its import illusive
dawn breaks
sunlight glares through mist
changing all living things
and eroding the rest
nourishing life
finally reducing it to dust

seeds of new beginnings emerge
day after day after decade
after century
after millennium
dawn breaks

Interruption

clouds are thick and frosted
lights somewhere behind
silvering the inconsistency
of their edges

twilight's curtains quiver
whispering thunder
shifting images

I stand alone
in a small square of light
framed by my kitchen window
and gaze up at the sky
listening to your words
intrude upon the silence
of my private patch of life

Goal

ahead of me
where the path widens
I approach carefully
timidly
fearfully

a large oak door
taller than tall
tall enough to touch a cloud

in the middle
of a forest of dreams
lacking a home
or a building
or even a wall
to support its mass

I can barely reach
the door knob
and brass is slippery

no I am afraid
a huge oak door
doesn't belong
in this place

my path shouldn't
end here
I'll try another way
before it grows dark

Age

pocket comb
and thin white hair
make a mockery of mirrors
turn yourself inside out
how easy
for youth is there
where no one can see

it's a fiction to forget
and so we take a huge
and dusty tarp
roll ourselves
into its folds
coughing and laughing
arms and legs flying
suddenly succumbing to terror
we can't get out

I've Lost It for the Moment

I'm blurred
sleepless in mood
sleepy in reality

out of harmony
uncertain of form and motion
the edges wavering

now I hear a faint buzz
and something like
a bird's thin chirp

I concentrate
on a reality
out of my view

and find within me
a sigh
and a wish
for clarity
to focus my thoughts
and guide me back

Time Changes

much said
and succinctly
so late
and lately relevant
to a mood
of sleepless wonder
as time springs forward
an hour is lost
somewhere
in our conscious struggles

Silence

I wander aimlessly
not hearing my own footsteps,
and look up at the trees.
music of their leaves
is too subtly whispered
for me to understand
for me to join in their conversation
and break the silence
still wrapped around me

The Far Side

the far side of the moon
is a mystery
to the temptations
and explorations
beyond a smile's
beguiling promise
and the stillness
where no air exists

if there is a roar
or even a whisper
smiles do not change
shadows do not fade
they are an illusion

In a Few Words

hush of gray

shyly spoken whispers

In a Few Words

CONTENTS

Seasons Come. 333

A Child's Plea 334

Moonstruck 335

Haiku Collection. 336

Cinquains 338

In a Few Words 340

Haiku into Tanka. 341

In Haiku Style. 342

Another Time 343

Finality 344

Lost Sense 345

Gray Dawn 346

End of Summer. 347

And Seasons Go 348

Seasons Come

Winter

snow painted mountains
mist shrouded pines shivering
pine needles crackle

Spring

blossoms decorate
freshly painted greenery
trembling with new life

Summer

bright flood of sunlight
bathing nests in molten gold
baby birds chirping

Fall

trees shimmer brightly
birds fly south before new storms
brown gold leaves remain

A Child's Plea

I sit by the fireplace
and hear a bird sing
somewhere up high
in the dark
above the ashes

someone told me
birds nest in the chimney
please please don't light a fire

Moonstruck

the moon is a shiny new penny
tossed on the sky's black oilcloth
I would pluck it twirl it
and make its magic mine

a glowing reminder
safe in my pocket
but how sad the night sky
without its lucky charm

Haiku Collection

ripples of ridges
in iridescent rainbows
echoing sea swells

cliffs shoreline refuge
circling eddies swallow sands
far off waters sigh

leaf-bare trees etch skies
crows seek shelter in sparse twigs
I search for green leaves

fragile wings tremble
colors hidden in closure
soon explode in flight

dawn shivers through mist
as night's curtain parts slowly
light spills into life

forest greens filter
sunlight struggles by each leaf
painted patterns change

darkening skies sigh
mist settles raindrops touch earth
growth begins again

thirsty longings parch
burning sands in rebellion
naked birds retreat

bird songs flutter down
in a circlet of high notes
greeting pale rimmed dawn

warm moist air hovers
over trees reaching skyward
still branches glisten

night shadows close in
softening flames of sunset
as sky colors fade

three blackbirds circle
etching their patterns skyward
change paths during flight

grass blades bend windward
making soft beds for egrets
white birds fly away

canyon walls shadow
shimmering waters whisper
sunlight slowly fades

bare branches reaching
silhouetted against gray
once brushed by bright birds

Cinquains
(Notes on Japanese Gardens)

swallows
skim leaves
arch through branches
cavort in greenery
feathered grace

bushes
crimson blooms
tremble with life
vibrant colors tempt bees
bougainvillea

water lilies
blossoms floating
visited by birds
present shelter to Koi
decorate ponds

family
ducklings paddling
proud parents and babies
creating circles in bright waters
ducks

azaleas
pinkish blooms
double frills float
enticing birds and bees
flowers

rocks
create shadows
challenge shallow waters
tranquility disturbed by eddies
unmoving presence in singing streams
boulders

In a Few Words

Embrace

sea and sand
embrace tenderly
and pull apart
reluctantly
as if their meeting
might never be
repeated

Injury

broken wing
uncanny instinct
swoops downward
sudden descent
gravity's victory
in sullen dusk

In the Moment

children cry
with real tears
honesty quickens their grief
and permits a raging torrent
free expression

1952

you and I
smoke and wine
soft sigh of cushions
scratchy record
and a baby crying

Haiku into Tanka

flowers strewn on graves
witness fields always silent
rifles weep with guilt
battlefields a memory
for those whose tears water grief

music weaves through leaves
strummed softly on thin branches
above trees' bass tones
we dance to illusive tunes
and waltz upon fallen leaves

lovers part quickly
thunder echoing above
knives of light rip sky
kisses linger on their lips
passionate hearts still beating

ancient fallen trees
slumbering on rock-strewn shores
beside mountain lakes
once proud patriarchs sleeping
peacefully upon stone beds

shrill notes of silence
neon signs struggling through mist
midnight clearing streets
fear remaining in dawn's light
longer shadows mystify

squirrel dusting branches
bushy tail against sharp twigs
climbing toward tree's top
scampering to reach treasures
undaunted purpose pursued

In Haiku Style

Irises

tall indigo sentinels
perched on dusty spikes
regal in summer's glow

Sunflower

sunflower stands tall
and dominates his brother
stalwart with effort

Clouds

hush of gray
shyly spoken whispers
predicting rain

Thunder

rumbles rock
echoing
then
eerie silence

Koi

golden dancers
in still waters
pricked by rain

Another Time

baby shoes are bronzed
pictures faded
no toys
strewn about
to shout at silence

Finality

illusions
truth
torn
reality
cutting
deliberately
carelessly
into
delicate
fabric

❦

Lost Sense

my glasses distort
smudged by neglect
until I no longer
recognize you
my lover

🌱

Gray Dawn

mist rising from the sea
sighs
a whispered plea
peaceful eyes
promise of silver
veils of secrecy
blending emotions
tranquil beginnings

End of Summer

summer's dusk
supports cloud sails
reflected in the bay of ripples
below

a lone farmer
weary and discouraged
caressed by autumn's arms
wanders homeward

nearby
wheat fields suddenly shiver
as the sky begins to fade

And Seasons Go

Winter

lifeless white landscape
blistering cold forms sparkles
reflecting fire's warmth

Spring

fields of gold greet dawn
silent blooms turn toward sun's light
dreams renew life's hope

Summer

endless drifts of sand
blazing in windless sculptures
tears still dry unshed

Fall

red gold brown dry leaves
creep along frozen pathways
bird songs are muted

Alphabetical List

of Contents

Alphabetical List of Contents

About the Author 355
Above Me 266
A Child's Eyes 46
A Child's Plea 334
A Conversation with Cindy 136
After Fifty Years 59
After-Party 296
Age 324
A Golden Moment 43
A Jewish Bride 55
Alexis at Thirteen 48
A Lone Fish 274
A Mother's Loss of Faith 299
And Disappear 319
And Seasons Go 348
Another Time 343
Any Way You Look at It 281
Appointment 89
Appreciation v
April Morning 271
Armando 131
A Teacher Mourns 153
A Time to Laugh and
  A Time to Weep 104
Author's Note 108
Autumn 76
Autumn Performance 244
A Visit 85
Awakening 102
A Wedding Dress, ... 56
A Word About
  My Grandmother vi
A Young Follower of Rock Groups 295
Beach Morning 258

Beach Party 1950 26
Beacon on Coast Highway 209
Bea's Wildflowers 232
Bernice 140
Betrayal 303
Billy 142
Blossoms in the Sand 98
Brother and Sister Pact 16
By the Flaming Lake 165
Candle 304
Candles 36
Can We Still Dance? 172
Canyon Lights 248
Carpool 110
Changing Tides 318
Changing Times 97
Childhood Collage 14
Christmas Carousel 37
Christmas Sale 195
Chronicle of a Clarinet 170
Cinquains 338
Clay Dancer 94
Cliff View 259
Climbing 32
Clock 316
Cloud Shadows 268
Clowns 317
Coffee 91
Coffee Cup 305
Colorado Cloud Paintings 240
Courtnie on a Carousel 47
Crescendo 237
Crimson 289
Dancing in the Shadows 169

Daniel. 148

Danielle 116

Daughters. 52

David at Eight. 51

Deana. 130

Death of a Child 298

Decades Rap on My Door 28

Deception. 285

Decisions 313

Dedication iii

Delia. 126

Desert Sketches 234

Desolation 308

Direction 306

Do Not Break the Circle. 150

Doors 284

Dora. 138

Dream 301

Dress Rehearsal 167

Eagle's Flight 255

Echoes 185

End of Summer. 347

Estella 132

Explanation 302

Exploring the Redwoods. 225

Eyebrows 290

Falling Leaves. 101

Fidel. 141

Field Trip to Watts Towers. 181

Finality 344

First Day. 114

First Grade Graduation 152

First Rainfall. 267

Flirt 288

Floodlights. 311

Folk Dancers' Celebration 168

Follow Me. 42

Forest Graveyard 224

Frankie. 121

Frozen in Time 206

Generations 40

Ghosts 192

Ginger 149

Gino 128

Goal 323

Gray Dawn 346

Grief. 73

Haiku Collection. 336

Haiku into Tanka. 341

Harmony 250

Hidden Canyon Lake 261

Homecoming 1949. 31

Horizontal Rain 270

Hospitality 62

Idaho December. 262

Identification 286

Identity 280

In a Few Words 340

Inertia 312

In Haiku Style. 342

In Mourning 71

Innocence. 54

Inspiration 235

Interruption 322

Invitation 159

In Writers' Workshop 63

Irises 11

I Try to Remember 72

I've Lost It for the Moment. 325

Japanese Gardens in the Rain. . . 252

Javier 117

Jennifer at Twelve 50

Joey 119
Join the Circle. 162
Julie 127
Karyn 134
Kathy 139
Labor Force. 187
Laguna's Shore 256
Later. 246
Legacy 8
Leonardo 125
Life's Changing Journey 66
(Life's) Journey
   Through the Redwoods 86
Lincoln's Statue, Washington DC. 207
Listen for the Laughter. 39
Listen, Teacher 109
Loneliness 78
Los Angeles Skyscraper. 188
Los Angeles Theater, Downtown. 200
Lost Lover. 84
Lost Sense 345
Love's Resolutions 58
Makeup 291
Manuel. 143
Maria 118
Mario 122
Maryland's Winter 263
Masks. 292
Max 129
Message. 307
Military Graveyard 314
Molly 146
Moods in Gray 238
Moonstruck 335
Morning 33
Mountain Stream in Winter 265

Musical Notes in My Life. 166
My Dancing Shoes Trilogy 174
My Own Towers in Pacoima. 186
My Pen is a Paintbrush 221
Mystery 254
Nadine 123
Nicole at Five 49
Night Winds 100
Noble Stance 227
No One Wears Tennis Shoes
   in Boston 210
Notes on a Metro Subway Tour . . 196
Nurturing. 10
October 245
Offerings 287
Once Upon a Time. 41
One Day I Will. 61
On the Street Where I Lived 202
On the Wings of Words iv
Opportunity 297
Painter's Dream 219
Pamela. 124
Partners 163
Pause in the Pageantry. 208
Pedro 133
Playground. 115
p.m. – a.m. 80
Politicians 309
Protest 310
Rag Bag 293
Rainy Days, Rainy Ways 64
Re-birth 112
Recovery. 103
Reflecting. 82
Regret 77
Relationships 283

Relatively 321
Remembrance 96
Retreat 226
Return in Winter 315
Reunion 249
Rose Avenue
  Venice Beach 1935 212
Sailing 27
Sand 9
School Bells 111
Search 282
Seasons Come 333
Senior Years 34
Serenity 87
Sheryl 147
Silence 327
Sky Tears 260
Solitude 79
Son 53
Spirit 60
Spring 269
Steps in Time 173
Survival 236
Tango 164
Teacher Cuts Class 113
Tell Me a Story 6
Temporary Waters 239
Tenacity 243
The Box 92
The Clowns Are Here 38
The Far Side 328
Then and Now 5
The Other Side of the Coin 300
The Path 74
The Pumpkin Patch 44
Thirteen 294

Those Who Dance 160
Time Changes 326
Time Turns 35
Tomas 135
Total Recall 279
Tranquility 253
Transparent 220
Twilight Meeting 242
Twins 120
Unforgettable 90
Vacant Lot, Lost Playground 13
View from My Kitchen Window . . 228
Visions of Color and Grace 272
Visiting Skirball Museum 204
Visiting Vermont 12
Voice of the Sea 83
Waiting for Dawn 247
Watts Towers of Triumph 182
What Do I Know 189
When I was Forty 24
When I Was Ten 18
When I Was Thirty 22
When I Was Twenty 20
Where Sea Meets Land 257
Whispering Gardens 251
Whispers 88
Who Rides My Yellow Pony 320
Window "Pain" 229
Windy Day in Chatsworth 230
Within a Frame 264
Yosemite, Once Home
  of the Miwok 222

About the Author

Lillian Rodich is a senior poet who resides in Chatsworth, California. Her writing possesses a wonderful combination of warmth, wit and wisdom — a gift that any reader or writer would cherish. Her soul speaks through her writing especially in poetry. The beauty of her work is rooted in a life-long love of writing and dance. Inspiration of dance provides the rhythm and footwork while careful choice of words provides color and costume to her well-crafted poetry.

The seeds of this beautiful gift were sown during her years as a dance student and in her studies at UCLA and UC Berkeley and further by graduate work at California State University at Northridge. A twenty-six year career teaching in LAUSD (Los Angeles Unified School District) still flourishes, as now retired, in her private classes teaching dancing and creative writing workshops (on a volunteer basis). It has been my privilege to be a part of some of these groups. Lillian leads with a gentleness that brings others to believe in themselves and grow with her. She is an inspiration to all who know her.

She is widowed and has three children and five grandchildren and a close extended family including nieces and nephews who are the light of her life. They all are her devoted friends as well as having unconditional love for her. Truly, they inspire and appreciate her. She is also blessed with large writing and dance families who inspire and encourage her and are loving friends.

Rita Keeley Brown

AUTHOR, CREATIVE WRITING TEACHER,
WORKSHOP ORGANIZER, MUSICIAN